Photoshop 7.0 Upgrade Essentials

Vicki Loader
Barry Huggins

friendsof

DESIGNER TO DESIGNER™

Photoshop 7.0 Upgrade Essentials

First published May 2002
Reprinted September 2002

Trademark Acknowledgments

friends of ED has endeavored to provide trademark information about all the companies and products mentioned in this book by the appropriate use of capitals. However, friends of ED cannot guarantee the accuracy of this information.

Published by friends of ED
30-32 Lincoln Road, Olton, Birmingham. B27 6PA. UK.

Printed in USA
ISBN: 1-903450-87-X

Photoshop 7.0 Upgrade Essentials

Credits

Authors
Vicki Loader
Barry Huggins

Technical Reviewers
Terry Boedeker
Scott Citron
Denis Graham
Dave Taylor

Proof Readers
Libby Hayward
Adam Juniper
Caroline Robeson

Indexer
Fiona Murray

Commissioning Editor
Luke Harvey

Technical Editors
Victoria Blackburn
Julie Closs

Author Agent
Mel Jehs

Project Manager
Simon Brand

Graphic Editors
Ty Bhogal
Katy Freer

Managing Editor
Chris Hindley

About the Authors

Vicki Loader   www.vickiloader.com

Vicki's early years were spent in South Africa. Now she is resident in rural village England, a stone's throw from the heart of London, where she divides her days between freelance training (to private companies or through a select number of high-profile London-based training concerns), and writing instructional books with friends of ED.

A new business venture this year has been the formation of UK Trainers Direct (www.uktrainersdirect.co.uk) – an association of top-level trainers who market their services directly to private individuals and companies. In her limited spare time, she maintains a web site which functions as an ongoing training site by providing trainees with links to training resources.

Whenever possible she pushes the boundaries of creative software on a laptop computer, while sitting in the sun at a Mediterranean street café or on a tropical beach. During these difficult times, Cava, champagne cocktails, foreign movies, music, and tapas bars sit tantalisingly close by.

Barry Huggins   **www.matrixtraining.com**

Barry left behind his days in international Commerce and jumped enthusiastically onboard the Internet at a time when it was a vague notion in the public imagination. He saw the potential of the Internet as a golden opportunity to marry his passion for art, design and creativity with the new developing technologies. His computer generated design however soon brought him back to the international arena, creating designs for clients in Japan, the USA, Italy and Portugal.

Barry now has his own training and consultancy company in London – Matrix Training – where he specializes in graphics and multimedia applications for both the Internet and print publishing. On the increasingly rare occasions when he is not working, he indulges in his other passions of scuba diving in warm waters and playing saxophone. But as he readily admits, the distinction between work and play is becoming increasingly hazy and he wouldn't change that for the world.

Photoshop 7.0 Upgrade Essentials

The File Browser and Workspaces   **45**

2

Contents

Appendix

Introduction

Introduction

This book will introduce you to all the new features of Photoshop 7.0 and ImageReady 7.0. Thorough explanations are given covering how the tool or new feature functions, and how it applies to real world usage. Techniques and workflows, and how implementations of the new features affect existing workflows – positively or negatively – are also discussed and assessed. Therefore it is not primarily a 'how-to' type publication, rather it has a 'what is this, how does it work, and how can I use it' approach.

The new tools are covered using a feature-based method – each new feature is introduced, explained and assessed in turn. Each chapter concentrates on a particular area of improvement, and each new tool is examined on an individual basis. You may be required to use skills and techniques that you're probably familiar with from your use of previous versions of the application.

This book can be used as a reference book, or worked through from start to finish. Pick out the features that you think will be most useful to you, or read it all to get a thorough overview of what version 7.0 has to offer you. Either way, you'll get the head start you need to quickly incorporate the new features into your existing work patterns, and stay at the cutting edge of Photoshop design.

Platform specifics

Photoshop users are as likely to be Mac-based as they are to be Windows-based, and for this reason, screenshots will be relevant to both platforms. Throughout the book, you will find that some chapters have Mac screenshots and others have Windows screenshots. Regardless of this, any keyboard shortcuts will be written with the Mac one first, for example:

- SHIFT+CMD/CTRL+OPT/ALT is the keyboard shortcut to reset your preferences. SHIFT+CMD+OPT is the Mac shortcut and SHIFT+CTRL+ALT is the PC shortcut.

All you need to know about this book

This book covers any and all additions or enhancements that are provided with Photoshop 7. To keep things as simple as possible we've only used a few layout styles to avoid confusion.

A few of the chapters have practical exercises included, and these will all appear under headings in this style:

Using the new tool

In the time-honored fashion we have numbered the steps of each tutorial, like this:

1. Do this

2. Then do this

3. Do this next, etc...

When you come upon an important word or tool for the first time it will be in bold type:

Use the **Healing Brush** tool to ...

We've used different fonts to highlight filenames, and URL's too:

`Picture.psd` and friendsofed.com

And finally, all our menu commands are given in the following way:

Image > Adjustments > Hue/Saturation

Files for download

To produce the results as shown, you may need to download the source files required for some of the exercises from our web site at www.friendsofed.com/code.html or you can use similar images of your own.

Support

If you have any queries about the book, or about friends of ED in general, visit our web site, you'll find a range of contact details there, or you can use feedback@friendsofed.com. The editors and authors will deal with any technical problems quickly and efficiently.

There's a host of other features on the site that may interest you; interviews with top designers, samples from our other books, and a message board where you can post your questions, discussions, and answers. Or you can take a back seat and just see what other designers are talking about. If you have any comments please contact us, we'd love to hear from you.

Chapter 1

Photoshop 7.0 Upgrade Overview

What we'll cover in this chapter:

- *System requirements for upgrading to Photoshop 7.0*

- *Introduction to major enhancements and additions*

- *Overview of all other changes made from Photoshop 6.0*

The latest release of Photoshop contains a vast number of new features and enhancements, many of which are not apparent at first glance. In this chapter, you'll get an overview of the new features and their functionality, whereas the remaining chapters of this book concentrate on illustrating in detail the use of these features.

Not every enhancement or new feature has been given its own chapter, as some of the changes or additions have been very minor. The following chapters are devoted to those enhancements that were seen to be the most important or caused the greatest change. For this reason, you are encouraged to read this chapter before looking at the individual features in detail to ensure you learn about all the changes, major and minor.

System requirements

Presuming that you have already purchased your upgrade to Adobe Photoshop 7 and are ready to start reading about all the new features, mentioning the system requirements might seem a little unnecessary. However, in case you are experiencing some problems running the application, determining that your system meets at least the basic requirements might be a sensible process.

Macintosh platform

- PowerPC® processor (G3, G4, or G4 dual)

- Mac OS software version 9.1, 9.2, or Mac OS X version 10.1.3

- 128 MB of RAM (192 MB recommended)

- 320 MB of available hard-disk space

- 800x600 color monitor with 16-bit color, or greater, video card

Windows platform

- Intel® Pentium® class III or 4 processor

- Microsoft® Windows® 98, Windows 98 Second Edition, Windows Millennium Edition, Windows NT with Service Pack 6a, Windows 2000 with Service Pack 2, or Windows XP

- 128 MB of RAM (192 MB recommended)

- 280 MB of available hard-disk space

- 800x600 color monitor with 16-bit color, or greater, video card

Operating systems compatibility

As indicated above, Photoshop 7 will work in Classic mode on Macs running Mac OS software 9.1 and 9.2. The application has been fully carbonized to run effectively on Mac OS X, taking advantage of the increased functionality of the new operating system.

On the Windows platform, the application has been optimized so that it can take full advantage of the functionality contained within Windows XP.

Resetting preferences

The locations of the Preferences files are now stored in the following folders on the listed operating systems:

- **Windows 98**:
  Windows\Application Data\Adobe\Photoshop\7.0\Adobe Photoshop 7.0 Settings

- **Windows NT**: WinNT\profiles\<username>\Application Data\Adobe\Photoshop\7.0\ Adobe Photoshop 7.0 Settings

- **Windows 2000 and XP**: C:\Documents and Settings\<username>\Application Data\ Adobe\Photoshop\7.0\Adobe Photoshop 7.0 Settings

The Application Data folder on the Windows platform is a hidden folder and not visible by default. If you do not see the Application Data folder, go to Windows Explorer > Tools > Folder Options > View *and check the option* **View Hidden Files and Folders**.

- **Mac OSX**: Macintosh HD\Users\Library\Preferences\Adobe Photoshop 7.0 Settings

For other operating systems use the finder to locate the Preferences files. To reset your Photoshop preferences you can hit SHIFT+CMD/CTRL+OPT/ALT upon startup of Photoshop instead of needing to locate the file on your hard drive.

Opening documents

Obviously when working in Photoshop, that very first step you take is either to open or create a new document. The most obvious enhancement is the addition of the **File Browser**.

Using the File Browser

In previous versions of Photoshop, actually deciding which image you wished to open was often a major exercise in itself. However with the introduction of the new File Browser feature, searching for that elusive image is made easier with the display of thumbnail previews on the right-hand size of the window and with the larger thumbnail in the left-hand section. Extra information included in the File Browser, which can help you decide which file needs to be opened, is in the details contained in the Metadata pane at the bottom left and the ability to display image thumbnails along with details in the Thumbnail pane.

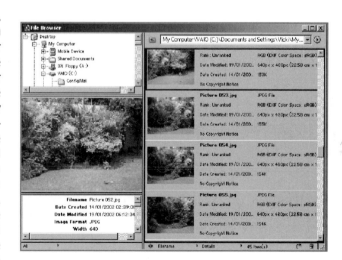

In addition to enabling you to search for your images visually using the thumbnails, the File Browser also allows you to execute a number of related file management functions, including renaming, rotating, and deleting files. The strength and functionality of the File Browser is detailed in Chapter 2, The File Browser and Workspaces.

Viewing merged data

Your layered Photoshop images can now be opened as composite images if you hold down the OPT/ALT+SHIFT keys when opening a file which has been saved in a format containing merged data.

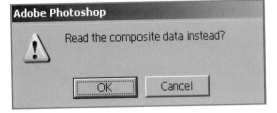

Using these keyboard modifiers sends a request to read and open the flattened composite data instead of the layered version. You can use this option with the following methods when choosing a file:

- File > Open,

- File > Open As,

- File > Recent Files,

- or if you are opening a file from the File Browser.

However, if you chose to disable **Always Maximize Compatibility for Photoshop (PSD) Files**, which is accessed through Edit > Preferences > File Handling, the composite data will not be saved with the file, and thus no merged data will exist. The converse implications of leaving this option checked will be discussed later in this chapter under the sub-heading **Maintaining Backwards Compatibility in PSD files**.

Unless you make any changes to the document, the File > Save *command will not be accessible. However, if you make a change and then save the file without changing the name or destination, you will be saving a flattened version of the file over your original layer file.*

Opening files with embedded profiles

Assuming that you are using Color Management to control the handling of Color Profiles and Profile mismatching, there has been a very important but subtle change in this version that may cause some frustration initially and cause you to make some changes in your workflow.

In previous versions of Photoshop, if you chose to discard or ignore embedded color profiles when opening a file, and then closed the file without making any further changes to the file, the file would close without a Save prompt.

However options have changed in this version. If you discard the embedded profile, even if you make no material changes to the file, Photoshop views this action as a change to the file and will always display the following prompt when you go to close the file.

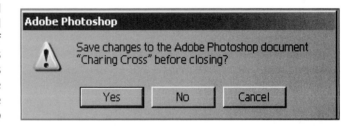

Although this may be confusing – in that you have not made any visible changes to the file – and irritating – especially if you have just opened a large number of files to have a quick look at them – by choosing to ignore or discard the Color Profile, Photoshop sees this as a change to the file in an attempt to stop you mistakenly stripping color profiles from files.

Unfortunately, however correct this approach is, it is going to cause some concern when you need to close all those files and you know that you have not made any changes to them. Two alternate workflows to overcome this could be to:

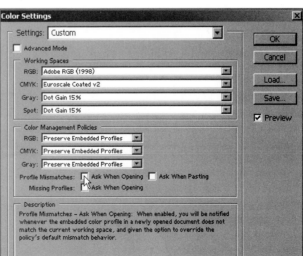

- Uncheck the options for coping with Profile Mismatches and Missing Profiles; and leave the Color Management Policies as **Preserve Embedded Profiles**. This could cause potential problems if you forget to reset your Color Settings options after opening and closing these files.

- Or by creating an action for opening and an action for closing such files and handling Color Profile problems, the process could be pretty much automated.

Customizing your Photoshop environment

We all work differently, have needs for different document sizes, different palette layouts, and different tool settings. In our individual workflow, we may find that we have a need to access these particular settings often. New features introduced in this release of Photoshop give us the ability to customize our environment, including the ability to create our own **custom document sizes**, **Workspaces**, and **Tool Presets**.

Creating custom documents

One of the first things you may notice when you create a new Photoshop document is that instead of having to type in measurements each time as you did in Photoshop 6, you know have access to what Adobe have determined to be preset sizes in common use. In Photoshop 7 a new field in the Open dialog box gives you access to these **Preset Sizes**:

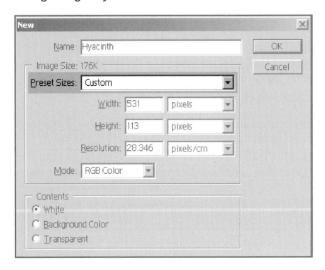

This is not the extent of its power – you have the ability to remove from this list any of those preset sizes which do not suit your particular workflow; and also to add your own custom sizes to this list.

Removing preset document sizes

The document containing the information about the preset sizes is called `Default New Doc Sizes.txt` and is located in the Required folder within the Photoshop 7 Application folder. Open this file in Notepad on the

Windows platform, Simple Text on Mac Classic operating systems, and on OS X use TextEdit.

If you are editing this file using TextEdit on OS X you need to choose Format > Make Plain Text *and then resave the file as* Default New Doc Sizes.txt. *This is to ensure that no formatting details are added to the plain text document.*

On opening the document, look carefully at the following points (part of the text has been included in the table below for your convenience).

- Some lines are preceded by a ";" (semi-colon). These lines are lines that have been remarked out, and therefore do not appear on the Preset documents drop-down menu.

- Document preset sizes are lines formatted as: **"Preset Name" Width Height Units** or **"Preset Name" Width Height Units Resolution**

  - Names of preset document sizes are encapsulated by quotation marks.

  - Width and Height are the decimal width / height of the preset, in units.

  - Units are the units for the preset and must be one of the following: pixels, inches, cm, mm, points, or picas.

  - If a Resolution value is not present, the resolution in the dialog box will not be changed. Otherwise resolution is print, screen, or an actual dpi or dpcm value, for example, 72dpi or 28.346 dpcm.

  - "separator" instructs Photoshop to display a separator line on the drop down menu.

    ```
    ; Version of the file
    1

    ; "Custom" will always get added first
    ; Followed by a separator

    ; Default document size
    ; Photoshop will calculate sizes based on
    the current system locale.
    ; This label indicates where in the menu the
    default size will go
    ```

```
"Default Photoshop Size"
"separator"

; Standard paper sizes

"Letter"     8.5    11.0    inches print
"Legal"      11.0   14.0    inches print
"Tabloid"    11.0   17.0    inches print
"separator"

; Standard picture sizes

"2 x 3"      2.0    3.0     inches print
"4 x 6"      4.0    6.0     inches print
"5 x 7"      5.0    7.0     inches print
"8 x 10"     8.0    10.0    inches print

"separator"

; Standard screen sizes

"640 x 480" 640     480    pixels screen
"800 x 600" 800     600    pixels screen
"1024 x 768"        1024   768    pixels screen
"468 x 60 web banner"       468    60     pixels
screen

"separator"

; Standard video sizes

"720 x 540 Std. NTSC 601"        720    540
pixels       screen
"720 x 536 Std. NTSC DV/DVD"     720    536
pixels       screen
"864 x 486 Wide NTSC 601"        864    486
pixels       screen
"864 x 480 Wide NTSC DV/DVD"     864    480
pixels       screen
"768 x 576 Std. PAL"       768    576    pixels
screen
"1024 x 576 Wide PAL"      1024   576    pixels
screen
"1280 x 720 HDTV 720P"     1280   720    pixels
screen
"1920 x 1080 HDTV 1080i"   1920   1080   pixels
screen
```

In modifying this preset file, I have decided to add the word inches to the document sizes under the heading Standard picture sizes to make sure that users who work in metric measurements are aware that these are inches. Also, I am going to add information on the resolution and remove the video preset sizes.

- To add the word inches, all that you need to do is to type it within the quotation marks, thus "2 x 3" becomes "2 x 3 inches 300dpi".

- To remove, but not actually delete the video presets, insert a semi-colon at the beginning of the line. Approaching it from this point of view means that if at any time you decide to restore the video settings, you do not need to type the details in again, you only need to remove the semi-colon from the beginning of the line. Consequently "720 x 540 Std. NTSC 601" 720 540 pixels screen becomes ; "720 x 540 Std. NTSC 601" 720 540 pixels screen.

- To tidy up the display of the drop-down menu, remark out the "separator" heading above ; Standard video sizes.

- Save and close the file, ensuring that it is saved as a plain text file with the name Default New Doc Sizes.txt in the P h o t o s h o p 7/Required folder. If Photoshop was open whilst you edited this file, you'll need to quit and restart the application.

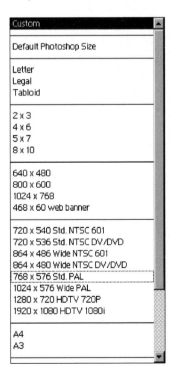
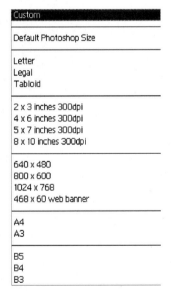

Note in the screenshot above, the additional details – inches and resolution - have been added, and the video presets no longer appear in the drop-down menu at the right.

Creating new preset sizes

Granted that the ability to customize the information which appears next to the presets and to remove presets that you do not often use is extremely useful, but then so is the fact that you can also add your own custom preset document sizes to this drop-down menu.

Consider the situation where you are designing a web site and all images on the site have to be one of three predetermined sizes. If each time you created a new image, you had to enter the dimensions and resolution in the New dialog box, this could be extremely time consuming. However, if those presets were available from the drop-down menu, you could save considerable time.

This could be completed in one of two ways:

- You could either add the details to the `Default New Doc Sizes.txt` file which was previously edited; or

- You can add the information to the `New Doc Sizes.txt` located in the Photoshop 7/ Presets folder.

For example, the following text has been added to both of the documents:

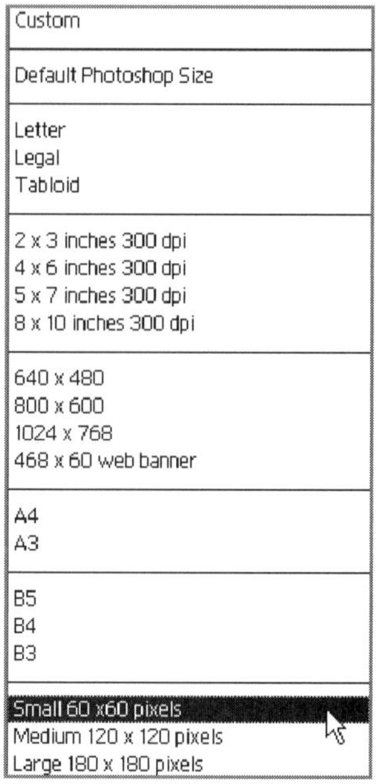

```
"separator"

; Henry's Web Images

"Small 60 x60 pixels"    60
60 pixels screen
"Medium 120 x 120 pixels"
120 120     pixels screen
"Large 180 x 180 pixels" 180
180 pixels  screen
```

Custom
Default Photoshop Size
Letter Legal Tabloid
2 x 3 inches 300 dpi 4 x 6 inches 300 dpi 5 x 7 inches 300 dpi 8 x 10 inches 300 dpi
640 x 480 800 x 600 1024 x 768 468 x 60 web banner
A4 A3
B5 B4 B3
Small 60 x60 pixels Medium 120 x 120 pixels Large 180 x 180 pixels

You'll notice the addition of the three new preset sizes at the base of the drop down menu. Although this new feature is extremely useful, you may find the need to edit the respective text files a little tiresome. Hopefully, future releases of Photoshop will provide us with the functionality to save a custom size from the New dialog box and to handle these custom sizes from the Preset manager.

Creating custom workspaces

Following on from the ability to create your own custom documents is the ability to create your own custom workspaces – or arrangements of palettes. The plethora of palettes within Photoshop often makes viewing your document difficult even if the Palette well has been used to store palettes, or the TAB and SHIFT+TAB shortcuts have been used to temporarily hide the palettes.

If you are spending a fair amount of time editing images, you may wish to create a palette layout which displays the Info palette, and the Layer, Channel, and Path palettes all separated from each other for easy access to the features on each palette. Arranging the palettes as you wish to see them and then choosing Window > Workspace > Save Workspace allows you to save the palette layout and then easily access it when required.

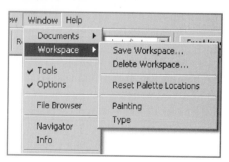

How to create, delete and manage these custom workspaces is described in more detail in Chapter 2, The File Browser and Workspaces.

Customizing tools

The ability to create your own Tool Presets is an additional feature allowing you to tailor the functionality of Photoshop to suit your own particular working environment. For instance, you might find that certain types of images react better to using the Healing Brush in Multiply mode, and others work better with a hard brush. Instead of having to change the settings of these tools each time you use them, you can create your own preset tools and then access them directly from either the new **Tools Preset palette** or **Tool Preset picker** each time you need them.

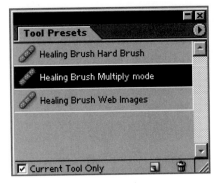

Using either the Tool Presets palette or the Presets Manager, you can create an unlimited number of tool variations to suit your own needs. The creation and management of these Tool Presets is discussed in detail in Chapter 3, Working with Tool Presets.

Using the new Painting Engine

The changes that have been made to the way that brushes are created, used, and managed is one of the major enhancements in this release of Photoshop. It marks a definite movement towards the more creative aspect of working within Photoshop where these brushes can be used to simulate traditional painting media in a way that was not previously possible. An excellent example of how these brushes can be used is shown in the Harvest.psd file that is located in the Photoshop 7.0/Samples folder.

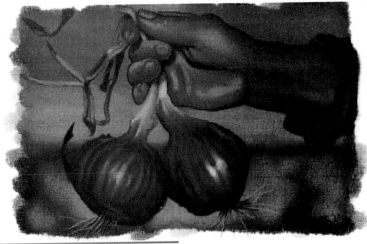

A further image which can be studied to show how these new brush features allow one to create images which look like they have been created using traditional painting tools and materials is the `Morning Glass.psd` file which is also located in the Samples folder.

These files illustrate very clearly how the brushes have been used both to simulate the use of traditional painting methods, and to introduce texture into the painting. In order to achieve this fine control, and almost infinite variety of brushes, the Brushes palette has been completely overhauled, redesigned, and expanded.

Notice how on the Brushes palette, you have options for adjusting the settings for the shape, tilt, spacing, scatter, jitter, diameter, texture, color, and other attributes of individual brushes, and you can even combine two brushes to create even further variations.

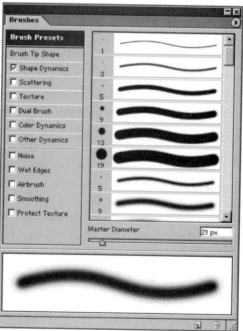

Furthermore these brushes can be saved as preset brushes using the Brushes palette menu and then managed or saved as sets using the Brushes option on the Preset Manager.

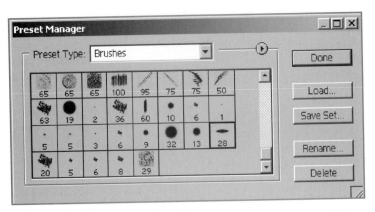

When you save a set of brushes, it is saved with the extension ABR. If you wish for these sets to be displayed at the base of the Brushes palette menu, for easy access, save them into the Photoshop 7.0/Presets/Brushes folder. Saving these files to disc means that you can transport them easily to different sites if you are a freelance designer' and you can also swap them with other designers.

Flow vs opacity

A further change to the Brush Tool options bar is the addition of a Flow button. Whereas **Opacity** is the maximum amount of coverage that paint can achieve in a single stroke, **Flow** is how fast the paint builds up during a paint stroke, or how fast it flows out onto the 'paper' with its limit being the current Opacity setting. You could liken the term Flow to what was Pressure in previous versions of Photoshop.

Note that when you have the Brush selected without the Airbrush icon depressed, using numeric values by entering numbers on the keyboard will change Opacity. If you have the Airbrush icon selected, or Airbrush is checked on the Brushes palette, changing the value via the keyboard will affect Flow instead.

Although the new strengths of the Painting Engine are discussed in more detail in Chapter 4, you'll get the most out of them by experimenting with the limitless variations.

The Pattern Maker plug-in

Another new creative feature introduced in Photoshop 7 is the **Pattern Maker** plug-in. Although the functionality to create simple patterns and textures has previously existed in Photoshop with the Edit > Define Pattern command, the options and control for creating variations of seamless patterns and textures is far greater with this new filter.

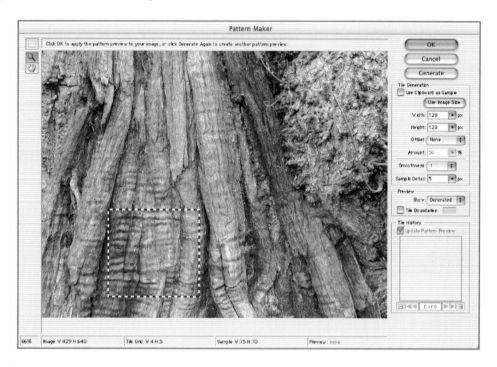

With the Pattern Maker, which is located at the top of the Filter menu along with the relocated Extract and Liquify plug-ins, you have the ability to create a number of variations from the same selected area, controlling the size and generation of the patterns. These patterns can then be saved as patterns to be used in backgrounds or even as textures in conjunction with the new Painting Engine discussed previously. An entire chapter, Chapter 5, has been dedicated to discussing how this feature can extend your creativity.

Enhanced Liquify options

The Liquify plug-in which was introduced in the previous version of Photoshop has been enhanced with the addition of a new liquify tool – the **Turbulence** tool – and navigation tools for panning the image and zooming in and out. Added to this, there are now unlimited undos available from within the Liquify dialog box, the ability to see how the 'liquified' image relates to the original image, and the new **Save Mesh** and **Load Mesh** options.

Although the new Turbulence tool adds to your creativity, the navigational tools make it easier to zoom in and pan to inspect details and the undos allow for those little glitches. The new Background features allow for more precise modifications, as you are able to see how the distorted image has been changed from the original or background. The feature with the most impact on the workflow is undoubtedly the ability to save and load meshes.

Saving and loading meshes have two distinct advantages:

- A modification does not have to be completed in one shift. You can start to distort the image, save the mesh, save and close the file and then continue with the image on the following day, by returning to the Liquify dialog box and loading the mesh.

- The ability to use a low-resolution file as a proxy file and then apply the mesh instantaneously to a high-resolution file. Modifications applied to the low-resolution file will be affected far quicker than if you were working with the high-resolution file, thus you can work quickly making the changes, then save the mesh and close the file. Opening the high-resolution file and then loading the saved mesh from within the Liquify dialog box will display the new file with the distortions immediately.

Discover how these new enhancements can improve your workflow and creativity in the in-depth look at the Liquify dialog box in Chapter 6.

Changes to the Layers palette and Blending modes

The Layers palette has been radically enhanced, both cosmetically with new 3D icons and the rearrangement of the Blending modes in what seems to be a more logical order; and with increased functionality in the form of new Blending modes, the new Fill option, and new Advanced Blending options.

At the simplest level, being able to double-click on a layer's name to change it is a welcome return to the options in versions prior to Photoshop 6. To access the Layer style and Advanced Blending options, double-click on the Layer icon on the palette.

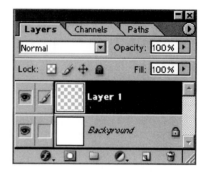

Changes to the Layers palette

Locking transparent pixels, image pixels, the position of pixels on a layer, and all aspects is now more direct. Instead of checking a check box next to the relevant icon, the icon itself is now depressed to activate the option and clicked again to release it.

Another new feature is the presence of a **Fill** opacity box, visible on the Layers palette itself. In previous versions of Photoshop, this Fill option was only accessible in the Advanced Blending options dialog box. Essentially the difference between Opacity and Fill opacity is that:

- Fill sets the opacity for the layer pixels, thus when you reduce the layer Fill opacity only the image pixel area is affected leaving any layer effects unchanged.

- Opacity sets the opacity for the layer pixels and any layer styles on that layer.

New Blending modes

Five new blending modes have been added to this latest release of Photoshop, **Linear Burn** and **Linear Dodge**, **Vivid Light**, **Linear Light**, and **Pin Light**, which are discussed in more detail in Chapter 7. You may also notice that the Blending modes have been reorganized on the drop down menu so that similar blending options have been grouped together.

New Advanced Blending options

New features enabling the use of Transparency, Layer Mask, and Vector Masks to further control the visibility of layer effects in advanced layer blending modes have also been added.

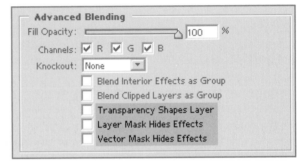

- Selecting **Transparency Shapes Layers** restricts layer effects and knockouts to opaque areas of the layer. Deselecting this option, which is always selected by default, applies these effects throughout the layer. In the illustration below, both rectangles have the identical Drop Shadow layer style applied to them. However, the image on the left has the default option of Transparency Shapes Layers applied, therefore the Drop Shadow style has been applied to the edges of the opaque square on the transparency layer. In the right-hand rectangle, this option has been deselected and therefore the layer effect has not been restricted to the opaque regions of the layer and is not visible.

- Selecting **Layer Mask Hides Effects** uses the layer mask to hide the layer and the effects rather than using the mask to shape the layer and the visibility of the effects.

- Selecting **Vector Mask Hides Effects** uses the vector mask to hide the layer and the effects rather than shaping the layer and the effects.

New Image Correction options

For the Photoshop user who spends a large percentage of their time retouching images for print and the web, the new features included in this release will more than justify the cost of an upgrade. The three new features – the **Healing Brush** tool, the **Patch** tool, and the new **Auto-Color** command – will make the task of correcting images far more time effective.

Using the Healing Brush tool

Similar in function to the Clone Stamp tool, the **Healing Brush** tool (J) comes with far more powerful options for retouching images. With the Clone Stamp tool, essentially one is cloning colors from one portion of the image to another, and although this option worked well in the past when handled with care, often a close inspection of the retouched area would show how the texture and color had been duplicated from one area to another. Furthermore with the Clone Stamp tool one had to choose the sample area very carefully ensuring that it was close to the target area in color, texture, light and shading.

With the Healing Brush tool, texture is sampled more than the color of the sample pixels. When the pixels are applied to the target area, the sampled texture is mixed with the color and luminance of the pixels surrounding that target area.

As with the Clone Stamp tool, the Healing Brush tool is used by selecting source pixels, using the Opt/Alt key, and then 'painting' these sourced pixels into the target area – the area to be retouched.

You may find that in using the Healing Brush tool, you will change some of your previous workflow options, such as cloning to another layer and leaving the original image area untouched as when retouching with the Clone Stamp tool. The Healing Brush tool cannot 'heal' to empty areas, but once you get your head around the concepts behind the Healing Brush tool, you'll be convinced of its strength.

Notice that the position of the Healing Brush tool on the toolbox occupies the space where the Airbrush tool was previously displayed. The changes to the Airbrush and how you can access its functionality are discussed under the heading *Missing Features* towards the end of this chapter.

The workings of the Healing Brush tool, along with tips and hints for using it more effectively, are covered in detail in Chapter 8.

The Patch tool

Allied with the Healing Brush tool is the **Patch** tool, which like the Healing Brush tool retouches areas. However there are differences in the way that the tools work making them more effective for use in different areas. If the damage to an area is too great, often using the Healing Brush tool will not totally remove the damaged area, and it is in these instances that the Patch tool might be more effective in covering up the damage.

Like the Healing Brush tool, the Patch tool also takes the texture, lighting, and shading of the area into account, but unlike the Healing Brush tool, the Patch tool applies the changes to a selected area.

With the Patch tool, you can either select the area to be retouched and then drag the selection to a 'good' area in the image – the area from which you wish to draw the pixels to correct the damage area. Or conversely, you can draw a selection around the 'good' pixels and then drag the selection over the area to be retouched.

Although similar in function, you'll find that you will use the Healing Brush tool more when you wish to paint in areas to be retouched and when the damage to the target area is not to extensive. You'll use the Patch tool when you wish to retouch entire selected areas at a time, and additionally the damage to the area to be retouched can be more intensive.

Further information and tips on how to use the Patch tool to retouch images can be found in Chapter 8, Enhancing Your Images.

Using the Auto Color command

The range of auto commands for color-correcting images has been extended with the addition of an **Auto Color** command.

Levels...	⌘L
Auto Levels	⇧⌘L
Auto Contrast	⌥⇧⌘L
Auto Color	⇧⌘B
Curves...	⌘M
Color Balance...	⌘B
Brightness/Contrast...	

Whereas the Auto Contrast command worked by making highlights lighter and shadows darker without affecting color. The Auto Levels option clipped the color channels independently consequently increasing the tonal range, and often removing color casts. The new Auto Color command looks for the average darkest and lightest pixels in the image, and uses them as the shadow and highlight values. Additionally it adjusts the midtones in the image so that those colors close to a neutral value are changed to the target midtone color.

As with all auto commands, the Auto Color command must be used with care, but with images that have an overall color cast, using this command does yield pleasing results.

Expanded Auto Correction options

An improvement to the Auto options within the Curves and Levels dialog box is an example of one of those enhancements not immediately apparent to the experienced Photoshop user.

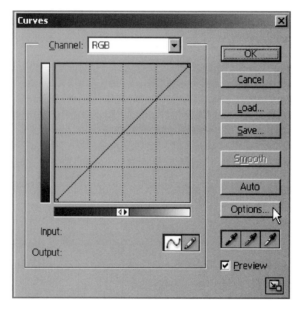

In previous versions of Photoshop, the options that could be set for the Auto command were limited to setting the clipping values used for the highlights and shadows when you chose the Auto option. Furthermore access to the Options screen was only possible when the OPT/ALT key was depressed within either the Curves or Levels dialog box.

Within the Auto Correction Options dialog box, you can now indicate how the tonal range of the image will be affected if the Auto option is used within either the Levels or Curves dialog box. Additionally the color values for the shadows, midtones, and highlights; and specific clipping values for the shadows and highlights can be set here.

The values specified within the Options dialog box can be used for one instance only or they can be saved as defaults for further Auto commands from the Curves or Levels dialog box, and when the three Auto commands from the Adjustments sub-menu are used.

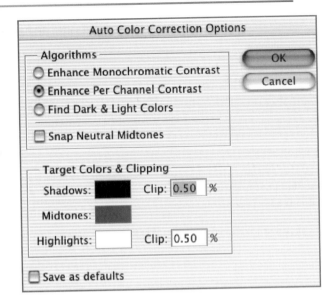

Read how to use the new Auto Color command and the enhanced Auto correction options to color balance your images in Chapter 8.

Optimizing and exporting web images

As design for the web becomes an increasing part of the designer's daily task, Photoshop has risen to the challenge by constantly improving and enhancing the way in which we optimize our images for the web and now also for the increasing number of portable devices in use today.

Selective optimization techniques for jpg images

Using the improved optimization techniques provided for saving jpg files for the web, it is now possible to set a different optimization setting for areas which may need to retain their crispness, including text layers, vector shape layers, and areas demarcated in saved channels.

Selective optimization techniques for gif images

Similar options are also provided for optimizing gif and png-8 images. There are now three options where text layers, vector shape layers, and alpha channels can be used as a mask, and the image quality and file size can be adjusted selectively. In each case clicking the small button next to the drop down box displays the **Modify Quality Setting** dialog box. Although the options are not new, the ability to use a mask is an enhancement.

Selective optimizing in ImageReady

ImageReady offers this function in the same way as Photoshop although there is no Save for Web option. Everything appears in the main window.

The **Optimize** palette provides access to the same settings as in the Photoshop Save for Web dialog box.

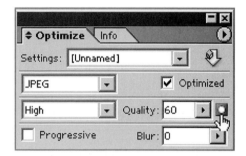

Whether you are in Photoshop or ImageReady, png-8 format is also available to use with masks and functions in exactly the same way.

Dealing with transparency

The need to create transparent areas in irregular web graphics has existed since the web began. The ability to create such graphics has been possible before now, however, with Photoshop and ImageReady 7, this process is simplified, increasing the speed of the production workflow.

Creating dithered transparency

Because web graphics are often placed over multi-colored backgrounds in web pages, or created with Drop Shadows which would appear unnaturally harsh when placed into web pages, this version of Photoshop sees the introduction of a dithered transparency option in both Photoshop and ImageReady. Although partial transparency is not yet an option in the production of web graphics, Adobe attempts to overcome this limitation and provide us with means of creating more realistic Drop Shadows by introducing the concept of **Dithered Transparency**. By mixing opaque and transparent pixels in a dithered pattern, this Dithered Transparency option creates the illusion of semi transparency.

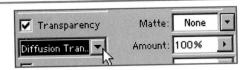

This option is accessible from the Save For Web dialog box.

Creating images in WBMP format

The increased use of hand-held devices such as cell phones and PDA's has generated a need for an optimized graphic format capable of delivering images to this growing audience. That format has now been standardized as WBMP (Wireless Bitmap) and is fully supported by Photoshop and ImageReady 7.

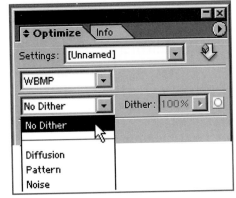

All the options for WBMP are accessed from Save for Web in PhotoShop 7 or from the Optimize palette in ImageReady.

These innovative features for generating robust images effectively are covered in detail with walk-through examples in Chapter 9, Optimizing and Exporting Images.

Creating rollovers in ImageReady

Previous versions of ImageReady allowed for the creation of rollovers without the need to hand code JavaScript. The implementation of rollovers in ImageReady was a little cumbersome because all the different states could not be viewed simultaneously. As well as slowing down workflow it made it very easy to make errors by applying effects to the wrong layers.

In ImageReady 7 this has all changed with the introduction of the new **Rollovers** palette. The Rollovers palette allows you to control all rollover states as well as gif animations and image maps all in one palette.

Changes can be made to different states by simply clicking on the state in the Rollovers palette and applying the required change. Furthermore, the new **Selected State** in ImageReady 7 allows you to make your web pages even more compelling with the creation of simultaneous rollover effects. Read more about these new features in Chapter 10, Creating Eye Catching Rollovers in ImageReady.

Improved text handling capabilities

Although the main focus of Photoshop is as an image-editing application, increased use in the design of entire web pages containing text and text-heavy print publications necessitated improving the text-handling capabilities of Photoshop

Check Spelling feature

Photoshop ships with a number of dictionaries, enabling the creation of multi-language documents and then the ability to use the **Check Spelling** feature to eliminate spelling mistakes in a number of languages in a single document.

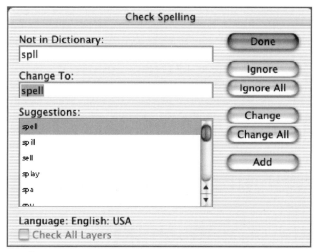

Using the Find and Replace command

In addition to the new Check Spelling feature, text handling functionality has also been enhanced by the introduction of a **Find and Replace Text** feature. This means that late-breaking changes in complex text heavy files can be effectively removed without the need for a manual search of the text within the document.

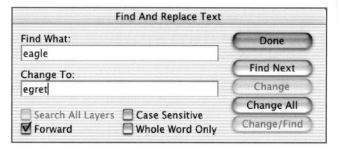

Although the above two features are the major new additions to the text-handling strength of Photoshop, there have also been a number of smaller refinements. These include the addition of a new text anti-aliasing option, easier access to some of the more commonly used character formatting options on the Character palette, and the introduction of discretionary ligatures with OpenType fonts. All these additions are covered in more detail in Chapter 11.

Increased functionality and productivity

Increased web production and the need to create new, updated web pages speedily has necessitated the development of tools which allow the user to concentrate on design and using additional tools to speed up that production process.

Enhanced Web Galleries and Picture Package options

While the production of Web Galleries is not a new feature to PhotoShop 7, it has been extended to offer a broader range of options including more templates for viewing galleries and greater options for providing information about the image, creator, or even general information. Most notably, this new information can include important security measures such as copyrights and watermarks, which can be automatically generated, helping you to prevent unlawful use of your images.

Picture Package production has also been enhanced with additional options, most notably the ability to let you print different page sizes, add labels or text such as copyright notices and captions to images, and also the ability to include multiple different images in one picture package.

The new enhancements to these two production tools are studied in Chapter 12, Creating Web Galleries and Picture Packages.

Scripting in Adobe Photoshop

The concept of automation was introduced to Photoshop with the arrival of Actions, and to some extent the ability to create and save Styles. This has been developed further with the release of an optional **Scripting Support** plug-in which will enable you to create and run cross-platform JavaScript scripts, AppleScripts for the Mac, and Visual Basic scripts for the Windows platform, which can be used to effectively automate repetitive process.

In Chapter 13, you are introduced to the concept of scripting within Photoshop and a discussion of the merits of adopting such an approach.

Working with Data-Driven graphics

Support for a data-driven production process has already been installed in the latest release of Illustrator; and the new **Variables** feature in ImageReady follows this direction by offering support for data-driven graphics, data sets, and variables.

Template designs can be created, and the objects within that design can be defined as variables. This means that by using applications such as GoLive or AlterCast in conjunction with these data sets and templates, new variations on web pages can be seamlessly and effectively delivered.

In Chapter 14, Using Data-Driven Graphics and Workgroup Management, the concepts of understanding and defining variables, and creating, modifying, and viewing data sets are introduced.

The concept of Workgroup Management with WebDAV

The growth of the tele-worker and other designers working from remote locations, coupled with large corporations using designers from within their local office or at remote branches means that in many instances files which are being developed need to be shared and managed.

WebDAV (Web Distributed Authoring and Versioning) is a server technology supported by PhotoShop that can be used to connect to a WebDAV server and from there manage files within the workgroup and prevent unintentional overwriting of files.

An introduction to the concepts behind WebDav is included in Chapter 14, Using Data-Driven Graphics and WorkGroup Management.

"Missing" features

Occasionally when you initially open a new version of your favorite application, it may look as if that tool or menu command on which you depended daily has been removed. Very often this is not the case, but you only realize that when you stumble upon the new location of the feature by accident.

The Airbrush tool

One of these 'missing' features is the relocation of the Airbrush tool and related options. The Airbrush tool has been removed from the Toolbox, and now exists on the Brush Tool Options bar. Notice the Airbrush icon that has been depressed to the right of the Options bar.

The related Airbrush options are accessed by clicking on the Toggle Brushes icon at the extreme right of the options bar, or by displaying the Brushes palette from the Window menu.

Once you have displayed the Brushes palette, depressing either the Airbrush icon on the Options bar as indicated above, or checking the Airbrush option on the Brushes palette will enable Airbrush style build-up effects.

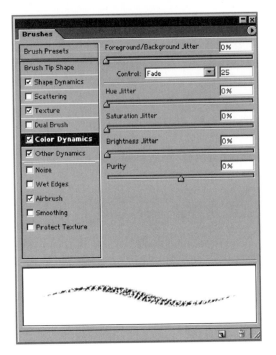

To simulate the previous Color and Opacity airbrush options, check Color Dynamics and Other Dynamics, set the Control to Fade, and insert the number of required steps. However, you are also able to control many other aspects of this new Painting Engine by using the Fade control in other options of the Brushes palette. So, although you may initially have thought that the Airbrush tool had disappeared, in essence it has been completely revamped along with the Paintbrush tool.

The Extract and Liquify plug-ins

Previously located at the base of the Image menu, these two plug-ins, which are essentially filters, have been relocated to the top of the Filter menu.

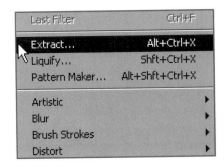

Saving files

Using advanced TIFF Save Options

In previous versions of Photoshop, the default setting for saving tiff files was that the file would be saved as a copy and layers would be ignored. A warning command at the base of the Save As dialog box would alert the user to the fact that some data – namely the layers – would be discarded, as is indicated in the screenshot below.

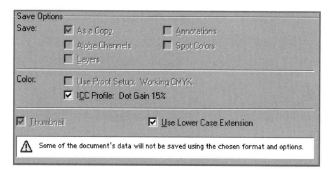

In order to save Advanced tiff files, the option under Edit > Preferences > Saving Files had to be checked as shown below. With this option checked, access to the advanced options and the ability to save layered tiffs was enabled.

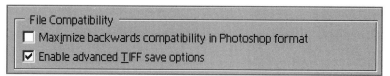

The workflow has been changed in Photoshop 7, where the default preference is set to allow layered tiff files, but to ask before layered tiffs are saved. Unchecking this option under Edit > Preferences > File Handling, means that if you have a layered file and you wish to save it as a tiff, no warning dialog box will appear to notify you that the file will be saved with layers.

When you save the file as a tiff, the Save As dialog box still has controls where you can indicate that you wish to save a flattened or unflattened version.

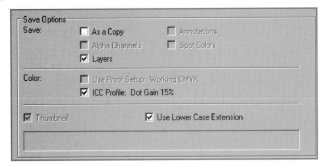

Unchecking the **Layers** check box, means that the option **As a Copy** is automatically selected and a warning that the "File must be saved as a copy with this selection" displays at the base of the dialog box. If you chose to save the file with layers, a further dialog box is displayed after selecting the tiff Save options, but this box can be forced not to display again.

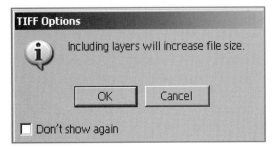

Whilst these changes may not cause any major mishaps in your workflow, and they offer a considerable advantage in that you can easily save tiff files with layers, three points should be considered:

- Saving layered tiffs will result in larger files, thus if file size is an issue you'll need to keep your eye on this.

- Unchecking the Ask Before Saving Layered tiff files and then opting that the dialog box above does not display again means that you could be saving layered tiff files without actually being aware of the fact.

- The majority of applications are able to access and read the composite data contained within a layered TIFF file if they are unable to open layered files. You would be well advised to check that your particular application is able to either open layered TIFFs or access this composite data.

Maintaining backwards compatibility in PSD files

In Version 6 of Photoshop, the option to "Maximize backwards compatibility in Photoshop format" was off by default, and modified only by accessing the preferences through Edit > Preferences > File Saving.

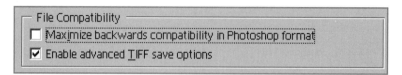

However in Photoshop 7, having the feature on has become a default setting, which can be changed by accessing the preference via Edit > Preferences > File Handling. In essence what happens when Maximize backwards compatibility is checked is that a flattened version of the file is saved with the layered file. The downside of this is the creation of large files, but the upside is being able to create files that are more compatible with other Adobe flagship applications, and being able to create a file containing both flattened and unflattened data. This means that should you decide to, you can open an unflattened PSD file as a flattened file by using the shortcut OPT/ALT+SHIFT when opening a file, a method discussed in more detail under the sub-heading *Viewing Merged Data* at the beginning of the chapter.

If you decide that you have no need to save a composite file with your unflattened file, you can switch off this preference. On deselecting the option, you will be confronted with the following dialog box, but you can opt not for the dialog box to display again.

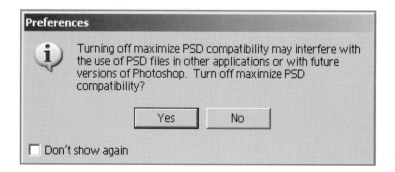

However, even if you opt not to have the dialog box display again, each time you choose to save a psd file with the Backwards compatibility option deselected, you will encounter a further dialog box.

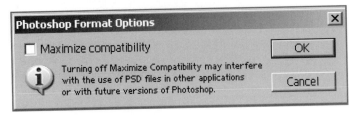

Enhanced pdf Save options

As the concept of pdf (Portable Document Format) becomes more and more widely used in both print and web workflows, Adobe have realized the need to ensure that files saved in the pdf format from Photoshop have the same level of **security** as files created in Adobe Acrobat. Thus the introduction of advanced security options on the Save As PDF dialog box.

Furthermore, to ensure that pdf files with embedded color profiles can be opened in the widest possible number of applications, a new option, **Downgrade Color Profile**, has also been added to the PDF Options dialog box.

Once the File > Save As option has been selected, and the format in the drop down menu is changed to Photoshop pdf, the next dialog displayed is the pdf Options dialog box.

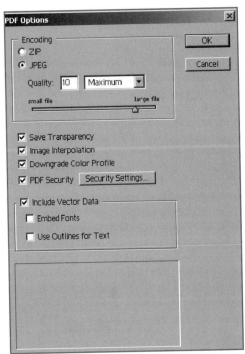

PDF security options

With the PDF Options dialog box displayed, checking the PDF Security option and then selecting the Security Settings button will enable PDF security for the file, and allow you to select the extent of the security options to be placed on the file.

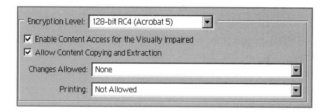

In looking at the PDF Security options dialog box, there are options to set either a **User Password** or a **Master Password**.

Setting User passwords

If you set a password for the User option, this password will then be required whenever the user wishes to open the document, in Photoshop or any other application which supports the opening of PDF files, including Adobe Acrobat and Adobe Illustrator.

If setting a User password is all that you intend to do in this dialog box, after you have entered the User password and clicked OK, you will be prompted to re-enter the password in an additional dialog box.

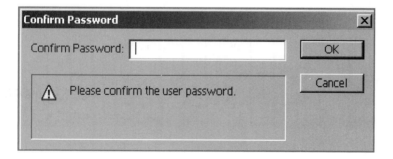

Note that if you opt to set only a User password and then give this password to users, they will be able to open the file in Photoshop and edit and print it as they would be able to with any standard Photoshop document. If you wish to ensure that this does not happen, you should also set a Master password which they will need to know if they wish to open the document in Photoshop, but not if they open the document in Acrobat – for this instance they will only need to know the User password.

Setting Master passwords

In addition to being required to open a document, setting a Master password is also needed if you wish to control the passwords and file modification permissions. If you have set both a User and a Master password, someone in possession of the User password would be able to open the file in any application supporting PDF files, but unless they knew the Master password as well they would be unable to change any of the permissions on the file.

As with the User password option, if you click OK after entering a Master password in the field provided, you will be prompted to re-enter the password in an additional dialog box.

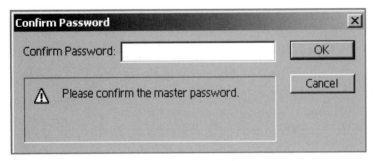

Choosing an Encryption Level

After setting either a User or Master password, you'll need to select an encryption level for the PDF file.

If you are unsure whether the persons opening this file will be using applications which support the latest level of encryption – **128-bit RC4 (Acrobat 5)** – you would be well advised to select **40-bit RCA (Acrobat 3.x, 4x)** encryption to ensure that the widest possible audience will have access to the file.

Dependent on which level of encryption you choose, different security opens are available for selection:

40-bit RCA encryption level

If you select 40-bit RCA encryption, the following security settings are available.

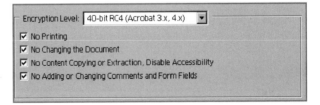

Remember that if you set only a User password, the file can be opened in Photoshop if the User password is known and the security options set below can be ignored.

Consequently we are presuming that you have set a Master password which is unknown to others, and the settings below relate to when the document is opened in Adobe Acrobat:

- Checking **No Printing** prevents users from being able to print the file.

- Checking **No Changing the Document** stops users making any changes to the document when the file is opened.

- Checking **No Content Copying or Extraction, Disable Accessibility** prevents users from copying text and graphics, and disabling the accessibility interface. The ability to disable an accessibility interface is only relevant if the document has been created as a specifically tagged document in Acrobat and therefore has little impact here.

- Check **No Adding or Changing Comments or Form Fields** to prevent users from adding or changing any comments (annotations) added during the creation process in Photoshop or from creating form fields.

128-bit RCA encryption level

Once again these security restrictions apply only to the file when it is opened in Adobe Acrobat. Remember that although these security options are available within Photoshop, some of the more complex options do not, as of yet, relate to Photoshop files.

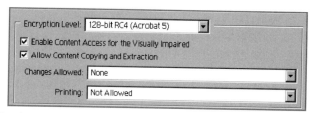

- Check **Enable Content Access** for the Visually Impaired to allow document contents to be used, which is required to support the Accessibility feature.

- Checking **Allow Content Copying and Extraction** will allow users to select and copy the contents of the PDF document.

- From the drop down menu under **Changes Allowed**, choose from the following options:

  ```
  None
  Only Document Assembly
  Only Form Field Fill-in or Signing
  Comment Authorizing, Form Field Fill-in or Signing
  General Editing, Comment and Form Field Authoring
  ```

  - **None** prevents users from making any changes to the file.

  - **Only Document Assembly** will allow users to create bookmarks and thumbnails in Adobe Acrobat.

  - **Only Form Field Fill-in or Signing** allows users to sign and fill in forms. This option is not really relevant to documents created in Photoshop.

  - Checking **Comment Authoring, Form Field Fill-in or Signing** will allow users to add comments to the PDF file in Acrobat.

  - **General Editing, Comment and Form Field Authoring** allows users to make changes to the file, comments and form fields within it.

- From the drop down menu under **Printing**, choose one to define the level of printing users are allowed:

  ```
  Not Allowed
  Low Resolution
  Fully Allowed
  ```

  - **Not Allowed** means that the document cannot be printed.

  - **Low Resolution** prints each page as a low-resolution bitmapped image. This can cause printing to be slow.

  - **Fully Allowed** allows the documents to be printed at any resolution. Note that in some instances allowing this option can leave a loophole which enables users to print the file in a format that they could then access and edit.

Opening a PDF with passwords in Adobe Acrobat

When the User password-protected file is opened in Acrobat, the following dialog box is displayed:

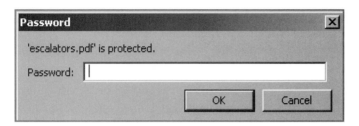

Any further access to the file will be prohibited until the correct password is entered. If a Master password, but no User password has been attached to the file, the user will be able to open the file, but they will not be able to change any of the security permissions which have been set for the file, neither will they be able to edit or save the file.

Never fall into the trap of setting security options without setting a Master password, otherwise all permissions can be changed and the file accessed and edited.

Opening a PDF with passwords in Photoshop

As mentioned before, if you save a PDF from Photoshop and attach only a User password, any security options attached will apply only to opening the document in Acrobat. Thus the user with knowledge of the password will be able to fully edit the file within Photoshop. On attempting to open a User password-protected file in Photoshop, the following dialog box is displayed, and the correct password will have to be entered before access to the document is allowed.

If a file which has both a User password and a Master password attached is opened in Photoshop, the following dialog box is displayed:

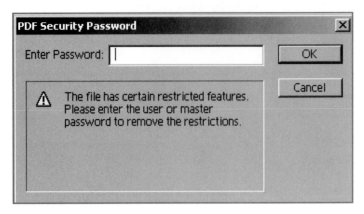

Entering the Master password directly will enable access to the file, but if only the User password is entered, a further security dialog box appears.

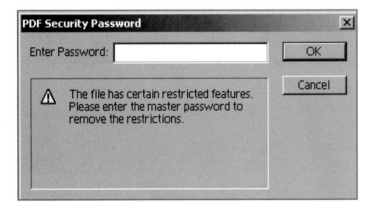

Attempting to open a file in Photoshop which has only a Master password and no User password attached, will display the following prompt:

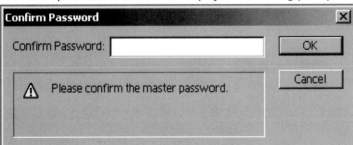

The addition of security features to the PDF File Save operation from within Photoshop will prove very useful to those companies and designers who need to provide the client with proofs of documents, or place PDF documents on the Internet; and yet still feel assured that the document is fully secured.

Conclusion

In this chapter you have been given an overview of some of the major new features introduced in Photoshop 7, and a closer look at some of the other enhancements. The rest of this book concentrates on looking at the various new features and major enhancements in detail.

Chapter 2

The File Browser and Workspaces

What we'll cover in this chapter:

- *Displaying the File Browser*

- *Using the File Browser as a palette or a window*

- *Opening files with the File Browser*

- *Organizing your files with the File Browser*

- *Customizing your Workspace*

As with any new features included in an upgrade, for them to be valuable, they need to satisfy at least one of the following criteria:

- *Do they make our workflow easier or more efficient?*

- *Do they allow us to work more creatively?*

*The new **File Browser** and the ability to create and save our own **Workspaces** are the new features that will be explored in this chapter, and they certainly fulfill the first of these criteria.*

The File Browser

The new File Browser feature allows you to navigate through folders, and displays thumbnails and information about the images in the folder you have selected. It makes locating the image that you want to use much easier than it is with the limited information available in the Open dialog box.

Using the File Browser also enables you to perform a number of related file management functions, including renaming, rotating, and deleting files. The extended functionality of the File Browser speeds up the process of locating and opening images, and allows you to manage your files from within Photoshop with greater efficiency.

Displaying the File Browser

You can display the File Browser options by:

- Clicking on the tab in the palette well at the top right of the screen.

- Selecting File > Browse.

- Pressing CMD/CTRL+SHIFT+O.

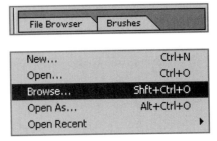

You can then choose to use it as a palette, or as a floating window – the way it works changes according to which option you use.

Using the File Browser as a palette

All the above options will open the File Browser as a palette, docked in the palette well. When it is accessed from here, it will automatically come to the front, hiding other palettes in your workspace. By clicking anywhere else in the workspace, for example, double-clicking an image name or thumbnail to open a document or starting work on an image you have dragged out, it will automatically close.

Using the File Browser as a floating window

If you want the palette to remain open while you work, you can detach it from the palette well by clicking the tab and dragging it into the workspace. You can also click on the File Browser tab, click ▶ to display the context menu and select Show in Separate Window. The browser will then display as a floating window behind the other palettes as you work.

You can move, minimize, or maximize it as you would any other window, but you can't bring it to the front of the other palettes by clicking on it. The best way to bring it into view is to use TAB (to hide the toolbars and palettes) or SHIFT+TAB (to hide the palettes).

To return the File Browser to the palette well, click 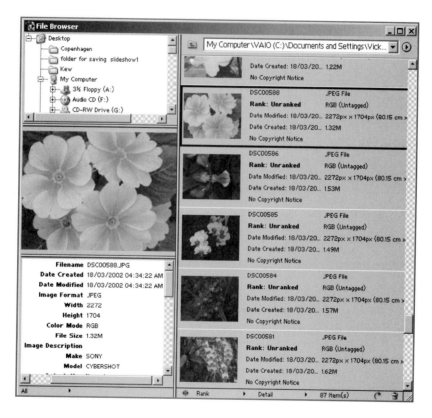 to display the context menu and select Dock to Palette Well.

Components of the File Browser

Once you have displayed the File Browser, you'll notice it is divided into four separate sections.

Clockwise from top left, they are:

- The **Tree View** panel – allows you to navigate through the folders and files on your computer. By clicking on a plus sign next to a folder you can reveal folders on the next level, and by clicking on a folder the contents of it are displayed in the Thumbnail panel.

- The **Thumbnail** panel – displays thumbnails of the images in the folder you have selected, sub-folders contained within the folder, and information about the files, depending on where you have navigated to, and the information display settings you have chosen. (See **Changing thumbnail displays**.) You can display the contents of folders here by navigating to them through the tree view panel or the drop-down menu at the top of the window.

- The **Information** panel – displays information about the file you have selected from the thumbnail panel. Again you have a choice about what information is displayed here. If there is no image selected the panel will be empty.

- The **Preview** panel – shows a larger preview of the selected image. If you have no image selected, or highlight multiple images, this panel will be gray.

Each individual component can be resized by hovering the mouse over the dividing lines until the two-headed arrow appears. You can also opt to make only the Thumbnail panel visible, by deselecting the Expanded View option in the context menu.

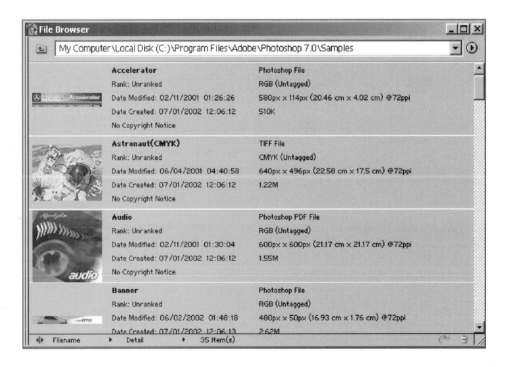

Using the File Browser to open a file or folder

When you have located the files you want to work on, you can open them by:

- Double-clicking the thumbnail of the image.

- Clicking on the thumbnail(s) to select and using the Open command on the context menu.

- Clicking and dragging the file / thumbnail onto the workspace.

All these methods allow you to open more than one file at once. The standard file selection shortcuts work here – hold down SHIFT and click to select multiple consecutive files, CMD/CTRL and click to select multiple non-consecutive files, CMD/CTRL+A to select all files, and CMD/CTRL+D to deselect all files. Alternatively the Context menu gives you the option to Select All or Deselect All.

If you are using the File Browser as a palette and you do not want it to close when you open an image, use these methods:

- To open a single file, double-click on the larger image preview on the left of the File Browser palette.

- If the palette is not in Extended View and the Image Preview pane is not visible, or if you want to open multiple files simultaneously, hold down the Opt/Alt key and double-click on the thumbnail.

If you select a file and then choose the Reveal Location in Folder command from the Context menu, the folder containing the selected image will be opened in Finder (Mac) or Explorer (PC).

Rotating thumbnail images

An added bonus is the ability to rotate the thumbnail images within the File Browser so that you can see the file at its desired orientation before you open it. To do this, highlight the target thumbnail image(s), and then click  at the bottom of the File Browser window-you can rotate multiple images if they are selected. Clicking once rotates the image thumbnail 90° CW, and if you hold down OPT/ALT, the rotation is 90° CCW. These options, and a Rotate 180° option, can also be selected from the Context menu.

When you rotate a thumbnail, the original image is not rotated until you open it. A warning dialog box will appear telling you this every time you click the Rotate icon, but it also has a handy Don't show again checkbox.

Note that if you choose to **purge the cache** at any time, these rotated thumbnails will return to their original orientation when you re-open the folder. See **Understanding the cache** for more details.

Controlling what the File Browser displays

You can customize what the File Browser shows to suit your needs using the following features.

Changing thumbnail displays

You can choose to display the image previews in five different styles, ranging from small, as shown in the screenshot below, to a large thumbnail complete with file information, as shown earlier. These **View By** states can be changed either by clicking ▶ to access the View By drop-down menu at the base of the palette, or by selecting the desired option from the Context menu.

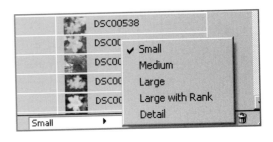

Obviously, choosing a larger option means that the thumbnails will take longer to be generated.

Viewing sub-folders

You can decide whether or not to display sub-folders in a selected folder by selecting/deselecting the Show Folders option on the Palette menu. Without this option enabled, only images will be displayed. When it is checked, you can double-click on a folder to open it and display its contents.

Accessing image information

Once you have selected a thumbnail, information about that image is displayed in the information panel. You can choose to display all available information on the image, or just the EXIF (Exchangeable Image File) information imported from a digital camera, (the date and time the picture was taken, resolution, ISO speed rating, f/stop, compression, and exposure time). Click to access the File Information menu and select the option you want.

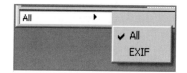

Organizing your files with the File Browser

Also, there is added functionality built into the File Browser that enables you to manage and organize many of your files from within Photoshop, eliminating the need for another program.

Organizing your files by allocating ranking orders

With the **Ranking** feature in the File Browser, you can give files a rank, and then ask that they are displayed in this ranking order. There are two ways in which you can assign ranks to an image:

1. Select the thumbnail image(s) you want to rank and then CTRL+click (Mac) or right-click (PC) to display the Context menu. Choose the ranking from the options at the bottom.

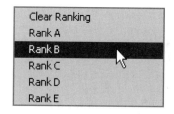

2. Go to the View By menu and select Large with Rank.

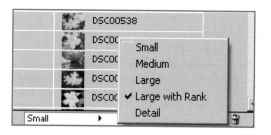

You can then edit the Rank field directly by clicking on it, and typing in up to 15 characters. Press the RETURN/ENTER key to complete the edit.

The second option offers more flexibility, but you can only rank one image at a time.

If you wish to retain any assigned ranking, you should perform an Export Cache command located at the bottom of the palette menu. We will discuss the Export and Purge Cache commands in detail a little later in this chapter.

Sorting the order of files in the File Browser

To re-order the files according to their newly assigned ranking, access the Sort By menu from the base of the File Browser and select Rank. Even if this is already selected, the File Browser will not automatically update when you amend an image's rank – select Refresh Desktop View (F5) from the context menu to reorder the files after making changes.

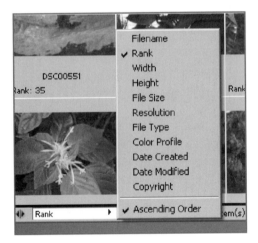

A slight peculiarity here is that if you do not assign ranks to all images within the folder, the files without a rank are considered by the ordering system to be higher ranking than those with. Also bear in mind that whilst you can give images ranks such as good, bad, or medium, the only order that the File Browser will recognize is alphabetical.

In addition to the ability to sort your files according to rank within the File Browser window, you have further ordering options available. To re-order the image thumbnails using another sorting preference, access the Sort By menu, and select one of the alternatives. You can also choose to check or uncheck Ascending Order.

Renaming files from within the File Browser

This feature is one of the strengths of the File Browser, and is especially useful when you have downloaded a number of images from your digital camera, or a stock library.

You can rename files or folders from within the thumbnail window using any View By mode. Click in the Name field, type in the new name, and press RETURN/ENTER to complete the edit.

You can rename a number of consecutive files or folders quickly by pressing TAB rather than RETURN/ENTER when you have edited a file name. This accepts the previous edit, and simultaneously highlights the next name field.

You can also rename files using the context menu.

Batch renaming files

This function saves time if you want to rename a number of files to form a set, perhaps pertaining to an occasion, venue, or subject matter.

To rename files, select the ones you want to rename, or deselect all to rename all files in the folder, and select Batch Rename from the context menu to bring up the dialog box.

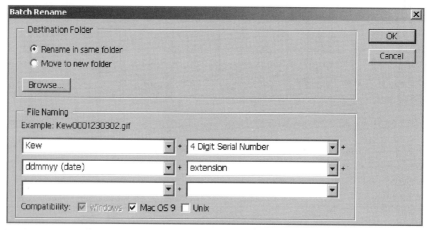

- **Destination Folder** – the options available allow you to rename the files within the same folder or move them to another folder. Click the Browse button to navigate to the target folder. This folder must be created prior to running a Batch Rename as you cannot create a new destination folder at this stage.

- **File Naming** – in the six drop-down fields, you can enter your own text or select the options. Everything you enter here will become a component of the new file name.

The options in the drop-down menu are:

- **Document Name** – this option will include the filenames already in use as a component of the new file names. You can choose from three capitalization options.

- **Serial Number** – selecting one of these options will mean that the filenames include a serial number generated by Photoshop. You can choose a number of digits up to four.

- **Serial Letter** – this will generate a letter rather than a number. You can choose whether the letter is capitalized or not.

- **Date** – this will include the date as a component of the new filenames. Note that this is the date you renamed the files, not the date they were created. There are various date formats to choose from.

```
Document Name
document name
DOCUMENT NAME
1 Digit Serial Number
2 Digit Serial Number
3 Digit Serial Number
4 Digit Serial Number
Serial Letter (a, b, c...)
Serial Letter (A, B, C...)
mmddyy (date)
mmdd (date)
yyyymmdd (date)
yymmdd (date)
yyddmm (date)
ddmmyy (date)
ddmm (date)
extension
EXTENSION
None
```

- **Extension** – this will include the file format extension. Selecting this option is a good idea to limit workflow hiccups when transferring files across platforms. You can choose whether you want it to appear in upper or lower case.

- **None** – this empties a field if you have previously entered an option you no longer want to use.

You can rename files using numbers with an arbitrary number of digits and also starting at a given value. For example if you enter 000123 as one of the name components, the names will have six digit serial numbers, and the numbers will be 000123, 000124, 000125, etc.

You must include one of the first three options, in order to make sure the filenames generated are differentiated. If you do not, a warning dialog will appear.

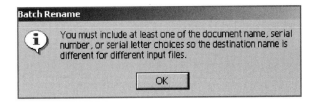

- **Compatibility** – checking this ensures that the files are named in accordance with the file naming conventions of various platforms, avoiding workflow problems later. There are three check boxes, for Windows, Mac OS, and Linux, although the platform you are working on will automatically be checked and grayed out.

Limitations

Note that within the Batch Rename function there is presently no support for renaming and copying simultaneously to a new folder. If you use this function you change the original files.

Also, the Batch Rename command does not offer support to automatically use part of the EXIF metadata generated by digital cameras as part of a filename, or a Search and Replace feature. However, as the File Browser is in its first incarnation, these are possible refinements that we may see in future releases.

Creating folders, moving, copying, and deleting files

You can organize your files from within the File Browser by moving and copying files into new or existing folders.

To create a new folder, access the context menu and select New Folder. (If you find this is grayed out, check that the Show Folders option is selected.)

Once the folder is created, type a new name in the highlighted field, and press RETURN/ENTER to accept the edit.

To move files, select the thumbnail images and drag them to the target folder. If you wanted to copy the files, hold down OPT/ALT as you drag. You can move and copy to folders displayed in the Thumbnail panel and the Tree View panel.

To delete a file, select it and do one of the following:

- Click on the 🗑 icon.

- Drag onto the 🗑 icon.

- Select Delete from the context menu.

- Press BACKSPACE (Mac) or DELETE (PC).

All of these options will bring up a warning dialog, but it does have a Don't show again checkbox.

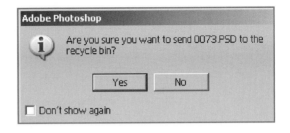

If you don't want to dismiss this box forever, you can avoid it displaying at certain times by holding down OPT/ALT as you delete.

Limitations

Note that the standard Cut, Copy, and Paste commands do not work from within the File Browser.

Although you can create folders from within the File Browser, you cannot delete them or move them.

If you delete a file you realize you need, you have to leave Photoshop to rescue it from your computer's Trash Can or Recycle Bin.

Understanding the cache

Each time you open a new folder, it takes a little time for the thumbnail images to be displayed in the right-hand panel. This is because the previews have to be built and saved into a cache. The upside of the previews being saved is a faster load time when you revisit a previously viewed folder. The downside is that this information is saved to disk, and if disk space is tight, this could cause problems.

To empty the cache and free up disk space, you can use the **Purge Cache** command in the context menu.

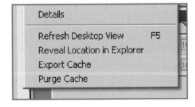

However, deleting this information means that you will lose generated thumbnails, and any ranking or rotation that you have applied. Also, this will cause thumbnails to be reloaded when you return to a folder, thus consuming processing time.

To preserve this information for a particular folder, you can use the **Export Cache** command. (Note that thumbnails must be generated before you export the cache, as it does not automatically update.)

When you export the cache, two files are saved in the folder, containing the cache information you generated while you were working in the File Browser. Although you can't see them in Photoshop, they are visible in Finder or Explorer.

AdobePS7.... AdobePS7.tb0

This means that any rankings or rotation are saved, along with the thumbnails, even when you purge the cache. You can move this information, along with the images, to an alternate folder, or even burn it onto a CD.

Customizing your Workspace

The ability to create and save custom palette layouts has become a feature in a number of applications, and this release of Photoshop sees the inclusion of this handy function in both Photoshop and ImageReady. With the plethora of palettes, and the very different workflows adopted by users within Photoshop, rearranging those palettes constantly to suit your working environment became a bit of a nuisance. Furthermore, if you're a freelancer having to work on different machines, saving your own custom Workspaces onto a disc and taking them with you to these different locations will save you time.

Creating a custom Workspace

Although discussion of this feature will be directed at creating and using Workspaces in Photoshop, the process and commands are exactly the same if you wished to create custom Workspaces in ImageReady. With the new **Workspace** option, it is possible to open and position needed palettes, and then save the arrangement as a custom palette layout, to be recalled at a later date.

To create a custom workspace, place your palettes as desired on the screen and then choose Window > Workspace > Save Workspace.

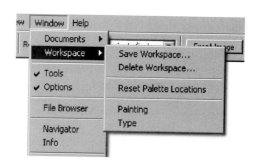

In the dialog box that appears, name the arrangement. This name will then appear on the Workspace sub-menu the next time it is displayed.

Using a custom Workspace

Once a custom Workspace has been defined and saved, it is easily accessed from the Workspace sub-menu.

Deleting a custom Workspace

Previously created custom Workspaces that you no longer need can be deleted by going to Window > Workspace > Delete Workspace. From the dropdown menu that appears, you can choose to delete either one selected Workspace or all of the Workspaces.

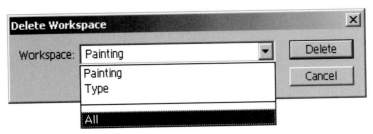

Should you find that you do not have an option to select and delete multiple Workspaces, then go to the Workspace files which are located in Library / Preferences / Adobe Photoshop 7.0 Settings / WorkSpaces / PSDir folder (Mac) or Application Data / Adobe / Photoshop/ 7.0/ Adobe Photoshop 7.0 Settings / WorkSpaces / PSDir (PC). From within this folder you could select to delete multiple arrangements. Locating this folder is not the ideal solution, but until such time as a Workspace option is added to the Preset Manager, this is the only way in which you can delete more than one Workspace without deleting them all.

On a PC, the workspace files may be in a hidden folder. If this is the case, you need to change the View settings (Tools > Folder Options) in Windows Explorer for the hard drive where Photoshop is located so that no files are hidden.

Conclusion

In this chapter we have introduced you to two of the new features designed to make your workflow more efficient – the new File Browser and the ability to create your own Workspaces. Although there are minor ways in which both of these features could be improved in future revisions, their inclusion in this release should certainly be viewed positively. It may do much to smooth the workflow in terms of finding, organizing, and working with files.

Chapter 3

Working with Tool Presets

What we'll cover in this chapter:

- *Introduce the new Tools Preset palette*

- *Ways of creating, accessing, storing, and sharing different tool presets*

*At first glance, the introduction of the **Tool Presets** might not seem that exciting. But on closer examination, you may begin to feel as I do about the feature – that it is groundbreaking and that it may even change the way in which we work in Photoshop, making the traditional toolbox pretty much redundant in our workflow. And if you couple this feature with the new brushes that we can now create (which is covered in Chapter 4), the ability to create and save tool presets really opens up Photoshop to the creative user in a way that has not been possible in the past.*

The Tool Presets option allows you to define the desired settings for a tool in a specific situation, and then save the settings as a preset. This can then be easily accessed and even shared with other users. This eliminates the need to re-invent the wheel each time you find yourself in the same situation.

Using this feature enables some degree of automation in the production of images, as presets can be used to access frequently used tool settings. For the creative painter it is useful for storing and re-using certain paintbrush settings.

Introducing the Tool Presets palette

Before we begin to use and create our own tool presets, let's take a quick look at the palette and palette menu.

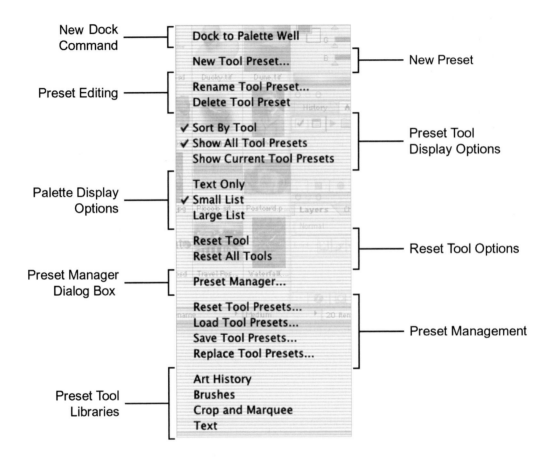

New Dock Command — Dock to Palette Well

New Tool Preset... — New Preset

Preset Editing — Rename Tool Preset... / Delete Tool Preset

✓ Sort By Tool / ✓ Show All Tool Presets / Show Current Tool Presets — Preset Tool Display Options

Palette Display Options — Text Only / ✓ Small List / Large List

Reset Tool / Reset All Tools — Reset Tool Options

Preset Manager Dialog Box — Preset Manager...

Reset Tool Presets... / Load Tool Presets... / Save Tool Presets... / Replace Tool Presets... — Preset Management

Preset Tool Libraries — Art History / Brushes / Crop and Marquee / Text

Looking at this palette, we can see familiar icons indicating options for creating New Presets, Deleting Presets, and accessing the palette menu.

The only unfamiliar feature is the option for displaying presets for the **Current Tool Only**. Checking this option will limit the presets displayed to those created from the tool currently selected in the toolbox. This can make it easier to find the one you want. (Note that if you pick a preset from the palette or picker, the related tool is automatically highlighted in the toolbox.) All other tool presets are hidden from view until the option is unchecked, or you select a different tool.

The Tool Preset picker is pretty much the same as the palette, the only differences being that it does not have a Trash Can icon for deleting tool presets, and the New Preset icon is located on the side and not at the base.

The Tool Presets palette menu

Moving our attention away from the actual palette to the palette menu, it is evident that Adobe has stuck with the consistent approach of trying to organize the common tasks together in sections. As we discuss the creating, saving, and management of tool presets, we'll look at the various sections in more detail.

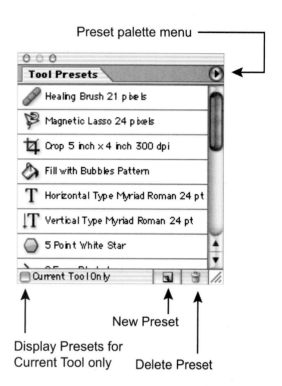

Preset palette menu

Tool Presets

- Healing Brush 21 pixels
- Magnetic Lasso 24 pixels
- Crop 5 inch × 4 inch 300 dpi
- Fill with Bubbles Pattern
- Horizontal Type Myriad Roman 24 pt
- Vertical Type Myriad Roman 24 pt
- 5 Point White Star

Current Tool Only

New Preset

Display Presets for Current Tool only

Delete Preset

Accessing predefined tool presets

When you install Photoshop 7, a number of pre-defined tool presets are loaded automatically with the application. You can access them by either clicking the button on the Options bar to display the new Tool Presets picker, or by using the new Tool Presets palette.

Brush: 13   Mode: Normal

The palette is located by default in the same location as the History and Actions palettes. As with other palettes, you can choose to drag it out to use it in it's own floating window.

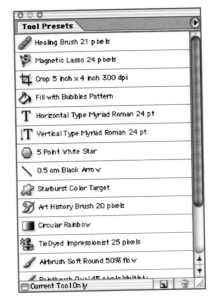

If you scroll down the tool presets using either the picker or the palette, you can see that a number of the standard tools have already been defined as presets, some with a few saved settings, for example the Rectangular Marquee 8 x 10. You'll also notice the existence of various creative Paintbrush and History brush settings. In addition, there are some presets for the Type tool – Photoshop does not support Type Styles as we know them from layout packages such as InDesign or Quark XPress, but by creating and saving tool presets, we can effectively simulate this feature.

To use one of these tool presets, or any others you have saved, simply select it from either the Tool Preset picker or the Tool Presets palette, and use the tool as you would normally.

There are also some other predefined toolset libraries. You can access these through the palette or picker context menu.

A dialog box will appear. Click OK to **replace** the current tool presets with those from the library you have selected, or **Append** to add the new tools to the current list.

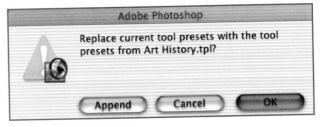

Creating and deleting your own tool presets

The real strength of this new feature lies in the power that it gives you to create your own customized tools specifically for your own workflow.

For example, imagine that the style guidelines for your website stipulate that each image has to be cropped to a precise pixel size. Using an earlier version of Photoshop, you would have had to enter the settings required in the Options bar of the Crop tool every time you performed this task. Alternatively you may have created an action to complete the crop, but this may not have given you the artistic control you desired. With the new capabilities to create and save presets, you can then simply choose the tool from your preset list and crop the images, knowing that they will end up with the size, resolution, and content that you need.

Creating tool presets

To create your own tool preset, select a tool from the Toolbar, Tool Preset picker, or Tool Preset palette. Define the desired settings in the options bar, and then choose the **New Preset** icon from either the Tool Preset palette or picker, or the New Tool Preset... command from either of the context menus. In the dialog box that appears, name the new preset and click OK.

Deleting tool presets

To delete individual tool presets, do one of the following:

- Select the tool preset on the Tool Preset palette, and click on the Trash can icon at the base of the palette. A dialog box will appear asking for confirmation.

- Select the preset and Opt/Alt+click on the Trash can icon.

- Drag the tool preset to the Trash can icon.

- Hold down the Opt/Alt key and move the mouse over the presets to display the scissors icon and then click on the unwanted tool preset.

- Ctrl/right-click on the target preset and choose Delete Tool Preset.

- Select the Delete Tool Preset command from the palette or picker menu.

Note that there is no Undo function here, and only the first option asks you for confirmation.

Renaming Presets

There are two ways in which a tool preset can be renamed:

- Highlight the target preset and choose Rename Tool Preset from the tool preset picker or palette menu, or by CTRL/right-clicking.

- Highlight the target preset in the Tool Preset palette and then double-click on its name to open the highlighted field for editing.

Controlling how the tool presets appear

As you create more and more tool presets, managing how and which ones appear on either the Tool Preset picker or the palette will become an important issue. You are able to control the contents of either by choosing the following options from the palette menu:

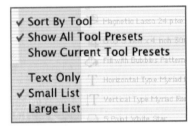

- **Sort By Tool** - re-organizes the loaded presets by tool. In other words all presets that have been created using the Paintbrush as a base will be ordered together on the palette.

- **Show All Tool Presets** - displays all the loaded presets on the palette.

- **Show Current Tool Presets** - displays only the presets relative to the tool currently selected in the toolbox. This is useful if your list of presets has grown. (Clicking the Current Tool Only button at the base of the palette also sets this option.)

- **Text Only**, **Small List**, or **Large List** - these change the way in which the presets are displayed.

Organizing tool presets from the Tool Preset palette

You can use the commands from the tool presets palette menu to control which set of tool presets are loaded, and to save newly created presets libraries. It is not possible to change the order in which tool presets appear other than by the **Sort by Tool** option on this menu. Should you wish to manually change the order this must be done through the Tool Preset Manager, which will be discussed in detail later.

Saving preset libraries

Once you have created a number of new tool presets, you may wish to save them as a library which can then be loaded again in future. Select Save Presets from the palette menu. The Save dialog box will then open and you can name and save your library.

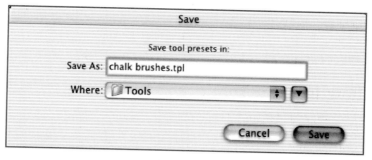

Note that when you choose to save from the palette menu, you cannot choose which of the presets to include. All of the presently loaded presets will be saved as a library, even if you have chosen to display only those based on the currently selected tool. You can always delete the ones you don't want before opting to save - if they are default settings they can be reset later.

You can save the presets anywhere on your hard drive. If you choose to save them in the Tools folder (within the Presets folder inside the Photoshop program folder), then the library name will appear at the bottom of the palette menu the next time you start Photoshop.

Tool presets are automatically saved with the extension .tpl. Should you wish to find the sets on your hard drive, copy and share them with others, or even make a copy of them to use on another of your machines, you simply need to look for files with that extension.

Loading preset libraries

If you have created a new set of tool presets or copied some from another machine, they can be loaded directly onto the Tool Preset palette or picker from the menu.

If you saved the library into the Tools folder as suggested above, and have restarted Photoshop since that action, then you will have access to the new library by choosing it from the bottom of the menu. Like those libraries that ship with Photoshop 7, you can choose whether to replace the current presets with those from the selected library, or add the new presets to the current list.

However, if the library is located elsewhere, choose Load Tool Presets from
the menu and navigate to the target file using the dialog box which appears.

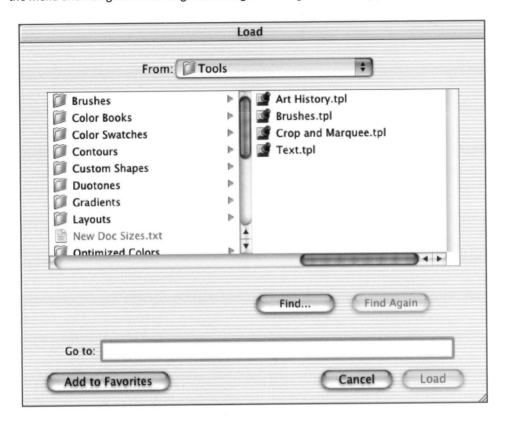

When you choose the Load Tool Presets command, the tools from the
additional library are automatically added to the end of the list in the
palette.

Replacing tool presets

The Replace Tool Presets command automatically removes the existing tool
presets from the palette and replaces them with presets from the chosen
library.

This is particularly useful if you organize your libraries according to certain
workflows. For retouching images, for example, you could create a library
containing a number of variations on the Clone Stamp tool, Healing Brush
tool, and Patch tool. When you had finished the retouching task, you would
no longer need these tools, and you could then replace them by loading
another library of presets, for example Type presets, rather than cluttering
up your Tool Presets palette.

Resetting the tool presets

If you wish to restore the contents of the palette to the default settings, choose the Reset Tool Presets command from the menu. Once again a dialog gives you the choice to replace the current presets or append the default presets to the list.

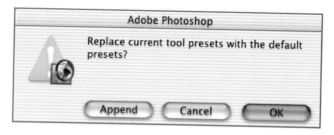

The default tool presets are located in the **Required** folder within the Photoshop program folder. If you want to create your own unique set of default presets, you need to save that file with the name `Default Tool Presets.tpl` inside the Required folder and choose Yes when you are asked whether you want to replace the file. It would probably be a good idea to save the standard defaults under a different name first as a back-up, in case you want to revert to them at a later date.

Using the Preset Manager to manage tool presets

Although the Preset Manager is not new to this version, the addition of the Tool Preset function means that its capability has been expanded to deal with this new feature. You can select it from within the palette or picker using the context menu.

As mentioned above, many of the tasks related to organizing tool presets can be managed from the Tool Presets palette or picker menus, but there are some additional options that can only be accessed from the Preset Manager.

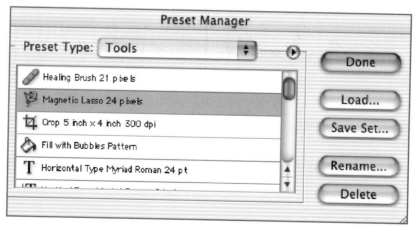

Reordering the tool presets

The actual order of the tool presets within the Preset palette can only be changed manually from within the Preset Manager. To change the position of a preset, depress the mouse over it and when the cursor icon changes into a closed hand, drag the preset to its new position within the stacking order, exactly as you would to reorganize layers in the Layers palette.

Note that if you wish to retain this order for the next time a particular library is opened, the set must be resaved over the existing .tpl file.

Saving preset libraries with the Preset Manager

When we discussed saving libraries from the Tool Presets palette and picker, it was mentioned that all the loaded presets are saved into a set even if they are not currently visible. With the Preset Manager, the options are different:

- To save all loaded presets as a library, ensure that no presets are selected and choose Save Set... from the dialog box.

- To save only a number of the presets, hold down SHIFT, and select the items you want to save, then choose Save Set... from the dialog box.

Note that this method isn't quite the same as the standard methods you may be used to for selecting files. While holding down SHIFT, you need to click on every file you want to be selected, not just the first and last, and if you hold down OPT/ALT you will see the cursor change to the scissors icon - if you click on a preset you will delete it, rather than select it.

Conclusion

The actual concept of being able to create your own tool presets might not initially seem a powerful feature, but when you start to think about how these tools could be created, reloaded, re-used, and even shared within your own particular workflow and environment, its strength really becomes apparent.

Chapter 4

Creating and Using Brushes

What we'll cover in this chapter:

- *Brushes palette viewing options*

- *Using Brush Presets*

- *Loading new palettes*

- *Modifying fixed and random settings*

- *Creating new brushes*

Photoshop 7's Brushes palette has undergone its most radical change to date. For the first time, the new Painting Engine allows users to simulate the effect of real media brushes. For the accomplished artist, this enables you to transfer all your skills from the canvas to the computer, and for the non-painter, it enables you to get in on the act and produce professional looking artistic work without the theoretical knowledge.

The brush types range from oils, acrylics, and watercolors through to pastels, charcoal, and crayons, but by mixing techniques there is no end to the styles that can be created.

Introducing the Brushes palette

As a preliminary to using the Brushes palette, the **Brush** tool (B) should be selected from the toolbox.

The Brushes palette can be found in the palette well at the top right-hand corner of the screen, or accessed from the options bar as in Photoshop 6.

Clicking the Brushes tab will expose the full palette. You can convert the palette into a floating window by clicking the Brushes tab and dragging it out of the well to any area of your workspace, to make it easier to examine the various options in the palette.

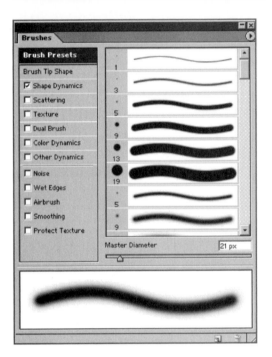

Options for viewing brushes

If it is not already selected, click the **Brush Presets** option in the palette.

This reveals the default brush selection in a scrolling list. At the bottom of the palette is a preview of the selected brush stroke.

The huge array of brushes in the palette can be viewed in a variety of ways depending on personal preference and available screen space. Click the pop up menu button in the top right of the palette to reveal the options.

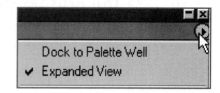

Make sure Expanded View is checked. This ensures all the information is visible.

The following viewing options are displayed:

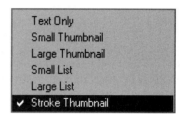

- **Text Only** – only the description of the brush is displayed.

- **Small Thumbnail** – the brush tip is displayed along with the diameter in a small icon.

- **Large Thumbnail** – the brush tip is displayed along with the diameter in a larger icon.

- **Small List** – the brush description is displayed along with a small icon of the brush tip.

- **Large List** – the brush description is displayed along with a large icon of the brush tip.

- **Stroke Thumbnail** – a small icon of the brush tip along with its diameter is displayed as well as a thumbnail of the actual stroke that will be produced.

Irrespective of which view is selected, a stroke thumbnail is always displayed at the bottom of the palette. This is usually the brush you have selected, but if you hover over another brush for a couple of seconds, you can then move the mouse up and down the list and the thumbnail will change accordingly.

Loading additional brushes

In addition to the default brushes loaded, there are additional brushes ready for you to use.

Clicking the pop up menu in the top right corner of the palette reveals the Brushes palette options once again. Selecting any of the following options will enable you to load a new Brushes palette:

- Load Brushes

- Replace Brushes

- One of the named brush sets at the bottom of the pop up menu.

Assorted Brushes
Calligraphic Brushes
Drop Shadow Brushes
Dry Media Brushes
Faux Finish Brushes
Natural Brushes 2
Natural Brushes
Special Effect Brushes
Square Brushes
Thick Heavy Brushes
Wet Media Brushes

When a brush set has been selected you will be offered a choice of how the brushes should be added to the palette. The options are to replace or append those currently loaded.

Adobe Photoshop

Replace current brushes with the brushes from Dry Media Brushes.abr?

OK   Cancel   Append

Appending the new brush set will add the new set to the bottom of the list. Note that adding too many brushes can make the palette unwieldy and difficult to manage, especially as there is nothing to stop you loading in the same set twice, to add to the confusion. Having a very large brush set also increases the time it takes Photoshop to launch from start up.

Once additional brush sets have been used, the default set can be reloaded by choosing the **Reset Brushes** option from the palette menu. Again, you will see a message asking if you wish to replace the current set with the default set of brushes or if you would like to append the current set.

If you would like to set your own defaults, you can replace the `Default Brushes.abr` file, located in the Required folder of Photoshop 7, although it would probably be a good idea to save the default set under a different name first, as a back-up.

Working with brush settings

Brushes can be set to react in a variety of ways, using random settings to achieve a natural hand produced finish. All the Brush Presets have been configured to act in a certain way. These settings can be overridden to achieve a different look and feel.

Click the Brush Presets tab to display all the preset brushes.

Click on one of the Brush Preset thumbnail previews to activate the brush you want to use.

Brush Tip Shape

Clicking the **Brush Tip Shape** tab displays all the settings defining each brush tip.

The Brush Tip Shape is the original piece of artwork that defines the brush shape. The brush tip in use for any preset brush will appear in the thumbnail list in the palette. The number beneath the brush tip icon refers to its diameter.

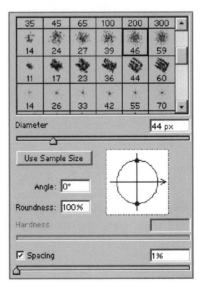

As with any other of the numeric settings in this dialog, the options can be changed by clicking the cursor in the field and pressing the up or down arrows. Holding down SHIFT changes the increment from 1 to 10.

- **Diameter** – this can be altered to increase or decrease the size of the brush tip, using the slider or the numeric field. The pixel size can be from 1px to 2500 px.

- **Use Sample Size** – this button returns the brush tip to the size of the original artwork. This button will not be enabled if the brush tip was not based on a sampled pixel area.

- **Angle** and **Roundness** – these settings control the shape and angle of the brush tip. You can use the numeric fields, or click the circle diagram and manipulate the circle as follows:

  - Click the arrowhead and rotate the circle clockwise or counter-clockwise to change the angle.

  - Click one of the black circles on either side of the main circle and drag towards the center to make the shape elliptical. Holding down the SHIFT key while dragging changes the amount in 10% increments.

  The Angle value can be between -180 to 180 degrees. Roundness is measured as a percentage, from 0 to 100 %.

- **Hardness** – this defines the size of the solid color center of the stroke produced by the brush. It is measured in a percentage value, from 1% to 100%. A high value creates a sharper edge, with a value of 100% creating a completely solid stroke, and a lower value softening the stroke.

- **Spacing** – this defines the distance between each brush tip shape. It is measured as a percentage, and the value you use can be from 0% to 1000%. Low values create one continuous line, while high values enable you to see each independent shape that makes up the brush stroke. At spacing values of more than 100% the individual brush tip shapes will be totally distinct from each other. When the Spacing check box is unchecked, the spacing will depend on how fast you move your cursor to draw the stroke.

Shape Dynamics

The Brushes palette offers a range of options for dynamically changing elements of the brush to create the feel of a randomly produced brush stroke. The **Shape Dynamics** option allows you to control the degree of randomness within the stroke as it is drawn.

Here, the brush stroke without Shape Dynamics (top) and with Shape Dynamics (bottom) are shown:

Click on the Shape Dynamics option in the Brushes palette to reveal the settings available to you.

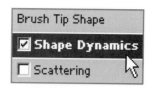

(Make sure you click on the actual word). If you only click the check box, you will enable the option without revealing the settings.

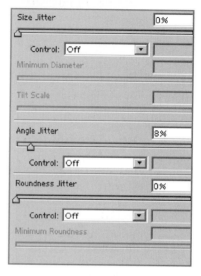

Let's look at the settings in detail:

- **Size Jitter** – **Jitter** refers to the amount of randomness applied to the option. In this case, **Size Jitter** defines the maximum amount that the size of the brush tip shape will vary as the stroke is drawn. The amount is determined by a percentage value. Moving the slider to the 0% position will not change the brush size at all, but setting the slider to 100% will allow the brush size to randomly vary by the maximum allowed value, resulting in a very irregular stroke.

  When Size Jitter is set to values of 1% or above the **Minimum Diameter** slider becomes enabled.

- **Minimum Diameter** – used in conjunction with Size Jitter, this option defines the minimum percentage amount to which the brush size can scale down. The percentage is based on the actual size of the brush tip diameter. So a 50% setting would allow a 60 pixel brush tip to reduce to no less than 30 pixels.

  The top line is a wide spaced brush stroke set to 100% Jitter and 100% Minimum Diameter, resulting in no size change. The bottom line is also set to 100% Jitter, but 50% Minimum Diameter, resulting in the brush tip that randomly scales down to a minimum of half the size of the original brush tip.

- **Control** – when set to Off, the size variance of the brush tip is controlled by the settings in the Size Jitter and Minimum Diameter sliders. Setting the drop down box to Fade allows you to fade the brush stroke from the initial diameter of the brush tip to the minimum diameter in a designated number of steps. Any number of steps from 1 to 999 can be designated and each brush tip counts as one step.

This brush stroke has Jitter set to 0%, Fade set to 10, and Minimum Diameter to 25%. The resulting brush stroke starts at the original brush tip size and reduces in size sequentially in 10 steps to the minimum specified 25% diameter.

An attractive tapered brush stroke can be achieved by setting the Minimum Diameter to 1%.

The **Control** drop down box offers three further options, which will only be enabled if you have installed a pressure-sensitive digitizing tablet such as the range produced by Wacom®. If you do not have a tablet installed, a warning icon appears alerting you that this option is disabled.

These options are **Pen Pressure**, **Pen Tilt**, and **Stylus Wheel** and will vary the size of brush marks between the initial diameter and the minimum diameter depending on the amount of downward pressure you apply to the pen, the angle of the pen, and the position of the pen thumbwheel.

- **Angle Jitter** – this defines the random amount that the brush tip will rotate within a full 360° radius. The angle of rotation is set as a percentage of 360°. Setting the slider to 0% will not rotate the brush at all. Settings of 100% will permit the brush tips to randomly rotate the full range from 0° to 360°. A setting of 25% allows the brush tip to randomly rotate a maximum of 90° from it's starting position, but as this is in either direction, there can be a lot of variation, and often a line produced using 25% Angle Jitter does not look that different to one produced using a 100% setting.

The Control drop down box below the Angle slider offers similar options to the Size Jitter control box.

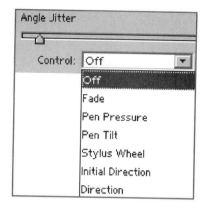

- **Off** – has no effect on the brush tip angle.

- **Fade** – allows the brush tip to fade between 0° and 360° in a specified number of steps. The number of steps can be typed into the numeric field next to the drop down box.

- **Pen Pressure, Pen Tilt, Stylus Wheel** – as with Size Jitter, these are only available in conjunction with a digitizing pad.

- **Initial Direction** – this maintains the angle of the brush based on the first brush stroke (See below).

- **Direction** – this changes the angle of the brush relative to the way the brush stroke is dragged on the screen (See below).

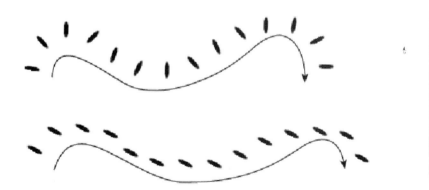

The top brush stroke was created with Angle Jitter set to 0% and Control set to Direction. The arrow illustrates the way the brush stroke was dragged. The bottom brush stroke was created with Angle Jitter set to 0% and Control set to Initial Direction. Again, the arrow describes the way the brush stroke was dragged.

- **Roundness Jitter** – this defines the random amount that the brush tip roundness will change. Setting the slider to 0% will not change the roundness of the brush at all. Settings of 100% will permit the brush tip roundness to change from the original size down to the size specified in **Minimum Roundness** slider.

- **Minimum Roundness** – this slider becomes enabled once the Roundness Jitter is set to any value from 1% and upwards. A setting of 100% maintains the original roundness of the brush tip. A setting of 1% causes the roundness to reduce to 1% of its original size resulting in a slim ellipse in the case of a perfectly round brush.

The top brush stroke was created with Roundness Jitter and Minimum Roundness both set to 100%. The bottom brush stroke was created with Roundness Jitter set to 100% and Minimum Roundness set to 1%.

The Control drop down box offers the same options as with Size Jitter:

- **Off** has no effect on the brush roundness.

- **Fade** fades the roundness of the brush between 100% and the number you have set in the minimum roundness setting over the specified number of steps.

- **Pen tool** options become available in the presence of a digitizing tablet.

Note that if you use this setting with an elliptical brush the results may be slightly unpredictable.

Scattering

Brush scattering defines the number and positioning of brush marks as you draw across the screen.

Click the **Scattering** option to display the options. When the word is clicked, the check box is also selected and scattering is then enabled.

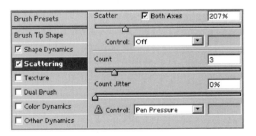

- **Scatter** – this defines the degree of scattering based on the percentage-based slider. A value of 0% produces no scattering, resulting in the standard brush stroke as it was created. Setting the slider to 1000% produces the maximum amount of brush mark distribution.

The boat on the left was drawn with scatter set to 0%, while the boat on the right has a scatter setting of 175%.

- **Both Axes** – this check box can be checked to produce scatter in a radial direction. This produces a broad area of coverage emanating from the brush's center. By deselecting the check box the brush marks are created along an axis at right angles to the line of the brush stroke.

The Control drop down box offers the same options as for earlier brush settings:

- **Off** has no effect on the brush scatter.

- **Fade** fades the scatter of the brush marks from the maximum amount of scatter that has been set to no scattering over the specified number of steps.

- **Pen tool** options become available in the presence of a digitizing tablet.

- **Count** – this defines the number of brush marks applied at each spacing interval, as a brush stroke is produced. You can choose from 1 to 16 marks. Whilst, in theory, it does not affect the spacing, the effect can make the individual brush tip shapes seem bigger, just as if you had repeatedly applied real paint to the same spot of the canvas, so the brush tip shapes may be less distinct from each other.

It also changes the effects of the other options. Angle Jitter with no scattering and a high count will result in irregular brush tip marks being produced, but probably less angle variation, as 16 randomly-angled brush tip shapes applied on top of each other will usually result in something approximately circular.

With a high scatter value, you can see how much denser the stroke becomes as you increase the count. This density means that especially if the brush you are using has spacing that has been set to a very low percentage value, the finished brush stroke will be made up of a huge amount of brush marks. This can decrease the painting performance on slower computers or if memory is limited. Higher values applied to the Count slider results in more brush marks.

● **Count Jitter** – this defines the amount of variation between the number of brush marks applied at each spacing interval. A higher percentage means more variation.

The Control drop down box works consistently offering the same options as previously outlined.

Texture

Applying the Texture option creates the illusion that the brush stroke has been painted over a textured background.

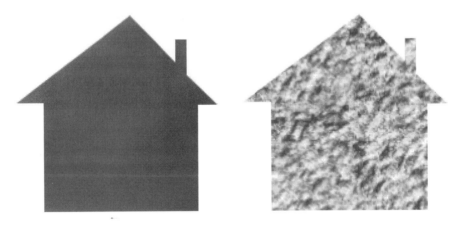

The house on the left has been painted using a brush without texture, and the house on the right uses the same brush but with texture applied.

Click the **Texture** option in the Brushes palette.

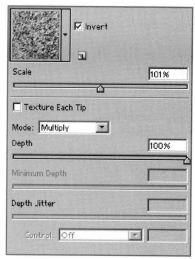

The thumbnail drop down box displays the current texture. Click the arrow on the drop down box to reveal other texture patterns.

- **Invert** – the illusion of texture is created by greater amounts of paint being applied to the lightest areas of the pattern and lesser amounts applied to the darkest areas of the pattern. When Invert is selected, this process is reversed thereby turning peaks into valleys and valleys into peaks.

- **Scale** – this reduces or increases the size of the original pattern by a percentage amount.

- **Texture Each Tip** - check this box to render the texture to each brush tip individually. This will result in a denser, more complex brush stroke. Selecting this check box enables further depth options.

- **Mode** – this defines the Blending mode to be used when combining the brush and pattern. You will recognize most of these from Photoshop's standard layer Blending modes, although some of them are new to Photoshop 7. If you are unfamiliar with these, a brief summary of the available blend modes follows as they relate to brush textures and the end result:

  - **Multiply** – always results in a darker color being produced.

  - **Subtract** – achieves a very high contrast effect.

  - **Darken** – lighter areas are darkened, while dark areas remain unchanged, overall producing a darker brush stroke than would have otherwise been created.

- **Overlay** – provides a more subtle effect in terms of the texture. Depending on the texture used it may only just be discernable.

- **Color Dodge** – contrast is reduced resulting in a much flatter, uniform brush stroke.

- **Color Burn** – increases contrast producing a more sharply defined, textured brush stroke.

- **Linear Burn** – this is a new mode to Photoshop 7. Overall brightness is reduced with an accompanying reduction in contrast. The texture remains strong, but a little muted in color.

- **Hard Mix** – another new mode, which produces a substantial brush stroke with strong defined texture mainly at the edges of the stroke. Overall darker.

- **Depth** – this controls the difference in relief between the high and low areas of the pattern texture, and consequently the amount of paint coverage. Setting the depth to 100% means that the texture has a lot of relief, so paint is only applied to the very highest points of the texture, and the pattern will be clearly visible when you paint with it. Setting the depth to 1% means your texture is very flat, so the paint will penetrate to all levels of the texture, and the pattern will not be visible in the resulting stroke.

- **Minimum Depth** & **Depth Jitter** – these two options become available when the Texture Each Tip check box is checked.

Minimum Depth defines a minimum amount of difference between the high and low areas of the texture. Depth Jitter affects the randomness of this variation in depth, the higher the setting, the bigger the variation.

The two settings work in tandem. Setting Depth Jitter to 0% will allow for no variance and so leaving the brush in its original form. A setting of 100% allows for maximum variance of the brush stroke.

Once the Depth Jitter has been set, the Minimum Depth can be adjusted. If you use 100%, the brush stroke should not be affected, and if you use 1% this allows for the maximum amount of variation.

The Control drop down box offers the same range of options as earlier for digitizing pads and fading.

Dual Brush

This option uses two brush tips to create brush marks. The main brush tip is defined in the Brush Tip section of the Brushes palette (see the beginning of this chapter) and the second brush tip is defined here in the Dual Brush section.

The following example shows a conventional single brush tip being used for the top brush stroke and the bottom example is the same brush tip with the Dual Brush option checked.

Click the word Dual Brush to reveal its options.

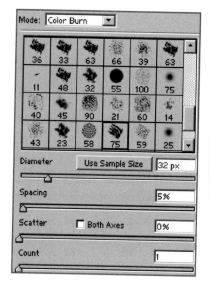

- **Mode** – this defines the Blending mode controlling the interaction between the two brushes. Once again these modes are taken from the Photoshop layer Blending modes (as explained in the **Texture** section).

- Brush tip thumbnail window – the list is the same as you will find in the *Brush Tip Shape* section. Here you can select the brush tip you wish to choose. If you are working with one of the preset brushes, a brush tip will already have been selected. This will be highlighted by a black outline appearing around the thumbnail.

- **Diameter** – this sets the size of the Dual Brush tip. The **Use Sample Size** button will only be enabled if the brush was originally created from a sampled area of pixels on the screen. When clicked, the brush will reflect the original sampled size of the brush. (See the **Brush Tip Shape** section for more details.)

- **Spacing** – higher percentage values create individual brush marks which are spread further apart. Lower percentage values create more densely packed brush marks resulting in a continuous brush stroke. (See the *Brush Tip Shape* section for more details.)

- **Scatter** – apply a high percentage value to create brush marks scattered further away from the center of the brush stroke as it is drawn across the screen. Select the Both Axes check box to distribute the brush marks in a radial fashion. Deselect the check box to distribute brush marks that are perpendicular to the brush stroke. (See the *Scattering* section for more details.)

- **Count** – defines the number of brush marks applied at each space interval in the brush stroke. (See the *Scattering* section for more details.)

Color Dynamics

The **Color Dynamics** setting is used to change the color of the brush stroke during the course of creating the stroke. The colors to be used are based on the colors currently set as the foreground and background colors in the toolbox.

Click the word Color Dynamics.

Set the foreground and background colors in the toolbox to colors of your choice.

- **Foreground/Background Jitter** – this setting defines the degree of color change between the two colors. At 0%, the foreground color is the only color used. As the percentage value of the slider is increased, the background color is brought into play. The higher the percentage value, the more the background color is used resulting in a wider variety of mixed colors based on the foreground and background colors.

- **Control** – the usual digitizing pen options are available in this box as well as the fade option, which fades from the mixed colors to the background color over a predetermined number of steps.

- **Hue Jitter** – this defines how much the color of the stroke can change. Lower percentage values change the color, but remain close to the color of the foreground color. Higher percentage values result in a wider range of colors being produced within the brush stroke.

- **Saturation Jitter** – this defines how much the saturation of the stroke can change. Lower percentage values change the saturation, but remain close to the saturation of the foreground color. Higher percentage values result in a greater difference in levels of saturation throughout the brush stroke.

- **Brightness Jitter** – this defines how much the brightness of the stroke can change. Lower percentage values change the brightness, but remain close to the brightness of the foreground color. Higher percentage values result in a greater difference in levels of brightness throughout the brush stroke.

- **Purity** – this controls the saturation of the color. At a value of -100, the color is completely desaturated resulting in grayscale values. At 100, the color is fully saturated.

Other Dynamics

This setting offers options for controlling the random Opacity and rate of paint flow for the brush stroke.

- **Opacity Jitter** – this defines the amount of randomness applied to the Opacity of the brush stroke. At 0%, the brush maintains the Opacity as set in the tool options bar. At 100%, Opacity varies by the maximum random amount up to the Opacity level defined in the tool options bar. The result is a stroke that varies in opacity.

- **Control** – the usual digitizing pen options are available in this box as well as the fade option, which fades from the Opacity value set in the tool options bar to 0 over a predetermined number of steps.

- **Flow Jitter** – this defines the amount of randomness applied to the paint flow of the brush stroke. At 0%, the brush maintains the flow as set in the tool options bar. At 100%, paint flow varies by the maximum random amount up to the flow level defined in the tool options bar. The result is a variation between faint and heavy brush marks.

- **Fade** – in addition to the same digitizing pen options, the fade option fades from the flow value set in the tool options bar to 0 over a predetermined number of steps.

Further options

The final options in the Brushes palette offer a simple check box that either enables or disables the effect. Check the box to enable the effect.

- **Noise** – this adds further randomness to the brush tips in a similar way to the noise filter. This option works best with soft edged brushes.

- **Wet Edges** – this option creates the effect of a build up of paint around the edges of the paint stroke in the same way that wet paint accumulates on paper.

- **Airbrush** – this enables the Airbrush option. This option has been available in earlier versions of Photoshop. The only difference is that it has now been removed from the toolbox. Selecting this check box also enables the Airbrush icon on the tool options bar. (You can also select the Airbrush option by clicking this icon.)

- **Smoothing** – this creates smoother curves when drawing brush strokes, particularly when using a digitizing pad. This option can also cause a short time delay, depending on the power of your computer.

- **Protect Texture** – when selected, all brush presets that have a texture will have the same pattern and scale applied. This is useful when you want to paint using a consistent canvas texture.

Creating new brushes

New brushes can be created from scratch or by modifying an existing preset similar to the way you worked in previous versions of Photoshop.

Creating a new brush from original artwork

1. Make a selection of the artwork from which you wish to create a brush.

I used the photo on the above left, located in the Samples folder shipped with Photoshop 7, as my starting point for the brush. After converting it to a 1-bit black and white image using the Threshold command, I made a selection of some of the palm fronds. The selection is pictured in the image on the right in light gray.

2. Go to Edit > Define Brush.

3. Type a name for the brush in the dialog box that appears and click OK.

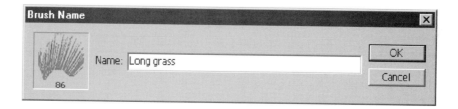

4. The new brush will appear in the brushes palette and any or all of the options discussed in this chapter can be applied to give the brush its unique characteristics.

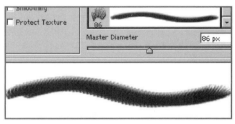

This is how the finished brush stroke looks when applied to the canvas. I left all the settings at their defaults.

The fine strands would have been tedious to create in other ways, but using an abstract element of an existing image made it simple. The brush was used to good effect in the meadow painting, pictured below. The dry brush effect was perfect for depicting the long wispy strands of grass.

Creating a new brush by modifying a preset

1. Select the brush you wish to modify in the Brushes palette.

2. Click the pop up menu button in the Brushes palette and select New Brush.

3.   Type a name for the brush in the dialog box that appears and click OK.

4.   The new brush will appear at the bottom of the Brushes palette leaving the original unaffected. Modifications can now be made using any of the options.

Saving brushes as tool presets

With the enormous selection of brushes available, it makes sense to save your favorites in an easy to access area. This is where tool presets come in. Any brush can be saved as a tool preset for quick access. See Chapter 3 on using tool presets for more details.

Using brushes with the Tool Options bar

The Tool Options bar, introduced in Photoshop 6, sees some small modifications relative to using the paintbrushes.

Most elements on the Tool Options bar are duplicates of other palettes.

- **Tool Presets** – any presets in the main Tool Presets palette will also appear here.

- **Brush Presets** – this provides the same information as in the Presets section of the Brushes palette.

- **Brush Paint Mode** – these are the same Blending modes from earlier versions of Photoshop along with a few new ones, which we will look at in Chapter 7.

- **Paint Opacity** – higher percentages make the paint less transparent.

- **Paint Flow** – higher percentages allow more paint to flow creating heavier coverage.

- **Airbrush** – this is the same Airbrush from earlier versions except it has now moved from the Toolbox to this new location.

- **Toggle Brushes palette** – click to open and close the Brushes palette.

Conclusion

In this chapter we have looked at the radically redesigned paintbrush. Spending a little time on experimenting with the various brush settings we have covered will open up the full potential and creativity of this powerful tool.

Chapter 5

The Pattern
Maker Plug-in

What we'll cover in this chapter:

- *Introducing the Pattern Maker*

- *Creating a simple pattern*

- *Fine-tuning the creation of pattern tiles*

- *Using the Smoothness and Sample Detail options*

- *Generating additional patterns*

- *Reviewing and saving pattern tiles*

*Although previous releases of Photoshop featured the Define Pattern command for generating textures and repeating patterns, the new **Pattern Maker** plug-in expands on this capability by providing for the creation of more complex textures and patterns. Essentially a filter, the Pattern Maker plug-in offers greater control and versatility when creating patterns for use as textured fills for your images, or for use as the basis of a new textured brush preset. With the plug-in you can create a variety of textures 'on the fly' and evaluate these variations before deciding whether to save them for future use.*

Although its usefulness may not be immediately obvious, it is a great addition to Photoshop. However this does not mean that the Edit > Define Pattern command is no longer of any use. You'll still find yourself using it for those simple patterns that you need to create quickly, and relying on the Pattern Maker plug-in to generate more complex variations of textures and fills.

How does the Pattern Maker plug-in work?

The Pattern Maker plug-in generates a pattern tile by reshuffling the pixels that are included in the sampled area of your image. Dependent on the settings that you choose from within the Pattern Maker dialog box, the resultant pattern can be a single tile covering the entire image area, or it can be a multiple of patterned tiles that fill the entire layer seamlessly.

Creating a pattern

To create your pattern, open the image you wish to use as the source for your pattern. This file must be an 8-bit image in RGB, CMYK, Lab, or Grayscale color mode.

Whenever you use the Pattern Maker, the entire active layer at time of launching will be filled with the generated pattern. If you wish to replace the image with the pattern then this poses no problem, however if you wish to retain the original image, you should either:

- Duplicate the layer before using the Pattern Maker, or

- Copy the source area for your pattern to the clipboard and then create a new layer or file to house the generated pattern. Note that your selection must always be rectangular in shape, and that you will need to use the Use Clipboard as Sample command in the Pattern Maker to access the source pixels that you copied to the clipboard.

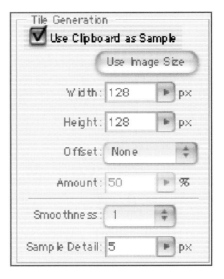

Furthermore, if you opt for this approach, you will need to click the **Generate** button, in the top right hand of the dialog box, before you see a sample of the pattern in the dialog box.

Creating a simple pattern

To become familiar with the basics of creating a pattern, you might wish to experiment using the following exercise as a base. Feel free to either download the sample file, `bark_LR.tif`, from the friends of ED website, or use a suitable file of your own.

1. Open the `bark_LR.tif` file, or a file of your choice. To safeguard any changes being made to the image, we'll generate the pattern using a duplicate layer.

2. With the duplicate layer as the active layer, choose Filter > Pattern Maker (CMD+OPT+SHIFT+X or CTRL+ALT+SHIFT+X).

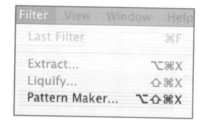

3. From within the Pattern Maker dialog box, use the **Rectangular Marquee** tool to sample a selection to be used as the pattern. Before you generate that first patterned tile, you can move the marquee selection, in order to sample a different area of the image, or make a new selection.

4. To create a simple pattern, ignoring for the moment the other refinements we can control in pattern generation, click on the **Generate** button (CMD/CTRL+G).

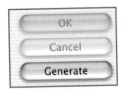

5. In the lower right hand corner of the dialog box, a sample of the tile is now visible in the Tile History preview box and the image has changed to reflect the new tiled pattern in the main preview area.

6. If you are satisfied with the initial pattern tile, decide whether to save the tile pattern for future use (this will be discussed in more detail later) or choose OK to return to the image. If you want to view another variation on the pattern, choosing **Generate Again** (CMD/CTRL+G) creates another pattern tile, reflected both in the Tile History area of the screen and in the main preview area. If you are not happy with the new pattern and prefer the original one, you can go back to it via the Tile History box, which we will look at in more detail later in the chapter.

7. On choosing OK you'll be returned to the main image where the duplicate layer has been replaced with the tiled pattern.

Note that the Pattern Maker respects any **Lock Transparent Pixels** options that have been applied to layers, so if you use an image with transparent areas that have been locked, these will not be filled with the pattern.

Generating a pattern from the clipboard

The other approach to generating patterned tiles while leaving the original intact is to copy a selection from the file to the clipboard before opening the Pattern Maker dialog box. The downside of this approach is that you do not have the freedom to choose another source area from which to generate tiles whilst within the Pattern Maker dialog box.

1. Using the same file as for the last exercise, click and drag with the Rectangular Marquee tool to create an area to be used as the source for the pattern. If you wish to hold down SHIFT as you drag to ensure that your selection is perfectly square in shape, you'll need to use this method, as the SHIFT and OPT/ALT keyboard modifiers do not work from within the Pattern Maker dialog box.

2. Choose Edit > Copy (CMD/CTRL+C) to copy the contents to the clipboard. Create and target a new blank layer in the file, or create a new file with the dimensions you want the final image to have.

3. Go to Filter > Pattern Maker (CMD+OPTION+SHIFT+X or CTRL+ALT+SHIFT+X) and notice that the image preview area is blank.

4. Select Use Clipboard as Sample to instruct Photoshop to generate the pattern using the clipboard contents.

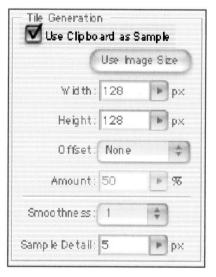

5. Click the Generate button and the Image Preview area and Tile History preview box will reflect the newly created pattern tile.

6. Click OK to return to the image or Generate Again (CMD/CTRL+G) if you wish to create another pattern tile.

Fine-tuning the creation of pattern tiles

In the previous exercise we concentrated only on the creation of the most basic of pattern tiles without paying any attention to the size, arrangement, or detail of that tile. The Pattern Maker options listed under Tile Generation in the dialog box give you the freedom to control these features.

Should you wish to generate one tile the same size as your image, click Use Image Size under the Tile Generation options.

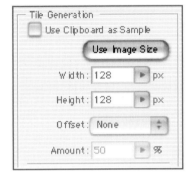

However if you wish to generate a series of patterned tiles smaller than the original image, you'll need to specify the Width and Height of the tile in pixels in the relevant fields as illustrated. Note that the size of the generated tile bears no relation to the shape and size of your original marquee selection. These two dimensions are completely independent of each other.

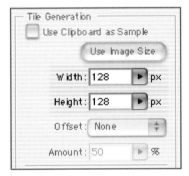

These tiles indicate how Photoshop generates a pattern dependent on the options chosen for the Width and Height of the resultant tile.

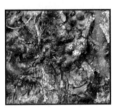

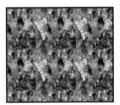

Original Source Single PatternTile Series of Tiles

The single pattern tile was generated using the Use Image Size command, generating one single pattern the size of the original image. In the right most picture, the width and height of the pattern was changed to 128 px and the result is a series of patterned tiles in the main preview area.

In addition to manipulating the size of individual tiles, you can also specify an offset value so that the tiles in the generated pattern are offset from each other, as opposed to merely stacking regularly. Both the Offset direction – Horizontal and Vertical – and the amount can be specified by choosing options in the relevant area of the dialog box.

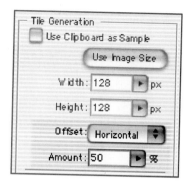

The top image shows a tile pattern with no offset applied, whilst the middle image has a Horizontal offset of 50 %. Note how in the second row of tiles, they have been offset 50% of the width of the tile, and resemble a brick wall arrangement. A similar value, in a vertical direction has been applied to the final tile.

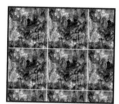
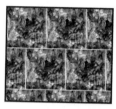
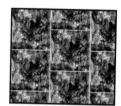

| No Offset | 50% Horizontal | 50% Vertical |

In the image above the pattern tiles have been demarcated to illustrate clearly how the pattern tiles have been arranged. By default, the tiles are simply arranged in the preview area without the visible divisions. However, should you wish to display Tile Boundaries, check the option in the Preview area of the dialog box. To change the color of the boundaries, click on the colored swatch to the right of the option.

Whilst you are using these additional options, keep an eye on the **Status Bar** at the base of the dialog box. It will keep you updated on zoom percentage, the size of the original image, the number of tiles which will be created both horizontally and vertically, the size of the original sample source, and finally, which tile preview is currently being displayed.

Note that while a pattern is being generated, you can press the Esc key to cancel it. This is particularly useful if you have chosen high Smoothness and Sample Detail options – discussed below – and are finding that the pattern is taking too long to generate.

Using the Smoothness and Sample Detail options

Although the default **Smoothness** and **Sample Detail** values will generally produce a satisfactory pattern, there will be times when changing these values will improve the results.

In this illustration, the tiled pattern on the left, created with a Smoothness value of 1, shows clear detail at the edge of each tile, so that it does not make the desired visually seamless pattern.

The pattern on the right was generated with an increased Smoothness value of 3 – the maximum – and the result is a smoother pattern with a marked decrease in the visible edges of each tile.

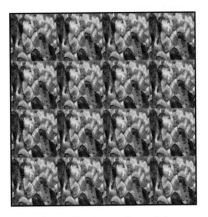
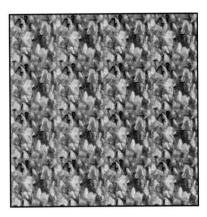

Smoothness value of 1   Smoothness value of 3

Similarly, if you find that your generated pattern tile does not seem to contain sufficient detail or that the detail that you wanted to feature within the tile is cut up, you may wish to increase the value in the Sample Detail field.

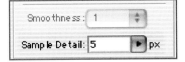

However, bear in mind that increasing either of these values will substantially increase the amount of time it takes to generate a tile.

Generating additional patterns

As mentioned earlier in this chapter, once you have selected your pattern source and generated that initial pattern tile, you are then able to continue generating variations using the Generate Again button, using either the same values and source, or making changes to those values and source pixels.

It is only possible to change the area that is being sampled if you have been working on a layer or duplicate layer that has pixel information on it already. You cannot change the source from within the Pattern Maker dialog box if you started with an empty layer or file and used the Use Clipboard as Sample option.

To change the sample area that is being used to generate the patterns, change the Preview Show option from Generated to Original.

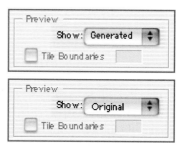

This changes the contents of the large preview area from showing the pattern to showing your original image, complete with the original selection marquee. This marquee can then be moved to sample a new area, or even redrawn. The new sample area will be used the next time you click Generate Again. There is no need to switch the preview back to Generated as this will happen automatically.

You can reset the image back to your original by holding down the Opt/Alt button. By doing so, the Cancel button will change to read Reset.

When you click Reset, your original image returns to the Preview area and the Tile History area becomes blank. You can then redraw or move your sample selection.

Whilst you are generating additional patterns, you can use the navigational tools to inspect the detail of the pattern more closely.

To zoom in on the pattern, select the **Zoom** tool (Z) and use it in the same way you would in the normal Photoshop image area. Note that your usual zooming shortcuts of Cmd/Ctrl+Spacebar and clicking, if you are using a different tool, Cmd/Ctrl++(plus) for zooming in, and Opt/Alt+Spacebar and Cmd/Ctrl+-(minus) for zooming out, also work in this dialog box. To fit the pattern preview in the window, use Cmd/Ctrl+zero.

If you have zoomed in on the pattern preview and cannot see the entire pattern, use the **Hand** tool (H), and click and drag on the preview to navigate to different areas of the pattern. Once again, the standard Photoshop SPACEBAR shortcut works here as well.

Reviewing and saving patterns

Each time you click Generate Again you are creating an additional alternative pattern. Up to twenty patterns can be stored and reviewed at any one time in the Tile History section. They can also be deleted and saved here.

At the base of the Tile History section, you'll notice the controls for navigating through the generated pattern tiles and the options for saving patterns as presets or deleting generated patterns from the Tile History.

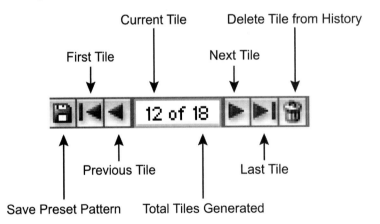

Note that as the maximum number of tiles that can be stored in the Tile History is twenty, if you attempt to create more than this, the original tiles will be replaced with the new tiles, with the oldest tile being replaced first.

- To navigate through the generated tiles use the video-type control icons to move through the tiles or type the number of the tile you want and press RETURN/ENTER. If you find that the redisplay of the tiles in the Preview area is taking a considerable time, uncheck the Update Pattern Preview option until you reach the desired tile and then check the option again. Doing this stops Photoshop from updating the preview area each time you select a different pattern tile.

- To delete a pattern tile, navigate to the target pattern tile and then click on the Trash can icon.

- To save a tile as a preset pattern, click on the Preset button. Note that when you save a tile as a preset, only a single tile is saved, rather than the whole pattern you see in the preview. Once you have saved a pattern as a preset, you can manage it through the Preset Manager, or use it as the basis for a pattern stamp or even a texture in your new brush options.

Conclusion

At first glance the Pattern Maker may appear to be just another fancy filter with little serious application. However, once you combine these generated patterns with features such as the new paint engine, tool presets, and even channels, you'll start to see the versatility of this feature. It is also a great tool for generating seamless textures for use in 3D applications.

Chapter 6

Using the Enhanced Liquify Options

What we'll cover in this chapter:

- *The new Turbulent Jitter option*

- *The ability to Load and Save Meshes*

- *The new Backdrop feature*

- *The new Zoom and Pan tools.*

Introduced in Photoshop 6.0, the Liquify feature has been further enhanced in this release, with the addition of three new tools to the Liquify tool bar – multiple undos, the new Backdrop feature, and the ability to save and load meshes. Whilst the new tools and Backdrop feature increase the functionality of this filter, possibly the most important enhancement from a workflow perspective is the ability to save and load meshes. Essentially this allows you to perform your initial manipulations on a low-resolution image and then save and apply that same mesh to a high-resolution version of the image.

The Liquify dialog box

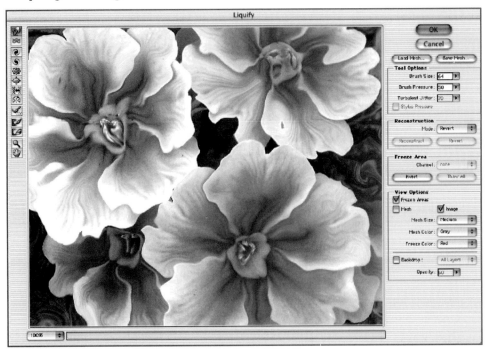

The first minor tweak to mention is the slight interface change – that the Liquify command has been moved from its previous position on the **Image** menu to the top of the **Filter** menu along with the **Extract** command and the new **Pattern Maker** filter.

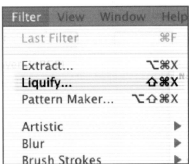

Navigating within the Liquify dialog box

Improving the way in which we can navigate and view our images whilst in the Liquify dialog box is attained with the introduction of the **Zoom** tool, the **Hand** tool, and the **Zoom Value** field in the lower left hand corner of the dialog box.

To zoom in on the image, select the Zoom tool (Z) and click, or click and drag, to zoom in on the pattern as you would if you were working in the normal Photoshop image area. Note that the usual zooming shortcuts of CMD/CTRL+SPACEBAR and CMD/CTRL++(PLUS) for zooming in and OPT/ALT+SPACEBAR and CMD/CTRL+-(MINUS) for zooming out work in this dialog box. Alternatively, choose a preset zoom view or enter your own value in the Zoom drop down menu at the lower left hand corner of the dialog box.

If you have zoomed in on part of the image, use the Hand tool (H), and click and drag on the preview to pan to different areas of the pattern. Once again, the standard Photoshop SPACEBAR shortcut works here as well.

Using multiple Undos

Another welcome addition to this feature is the introduction of multiple undos. No longer are you restricted to the standard CMD/CTRL+Z to undo your last edit, or using OPT/ALT and clicking on the Cancel button to reset both tool and image modifications.

Introduced in recent releases, the **Step Backward** (CMD/CTRL+OPT/ALT+Z) and **Step Forward** shortcuts (CMD/CTRL+SHIFT+Z) can now be used effectively from within the Liquify dialog box. Bear in mind when accessing this feature that the menu commands for Step Backward and Step Forward are not available from within the dialog box, so you have to use the keyboard shortcuts.

Introducing the new Turbulence tool

In the beginning of this chapter, we mentioned that three tools had been added to the Liquify dialog box. The Zoom and Hand tools were covered in the section on *Navigating within the Liquify Dialog box*, and in this section, we'll discuss the one true creative tool added to the options – the **Turbulence**

Useful for creating smoke, fire, and cloud effects, and for introducing a more painterly impression in images, the Turbulence tool works by mixing up the pixels directly below the brush head. The tool can be used either by continuously depressing the cursor over an area in the image, or by clicking and dragging to mix the pixels. In the illustration below, with the settings constant for the two modified instances, the middle image shows the effect of clicking, but not dragging, whilst the image on the right shows the effect of clicking and dragging with the Turbulence tool. Of course, dependent on your settings, your results will be quite different.

In addition to the usual options that dictate how the tool will react – Brush Size and Brush Pressure – the Turbulence tool has an additional option, **Turbulent Jitter**. The term **Jitter** refers to the amount of randomness that is applied to an element, with 0% being the minimum amount of randomness applied, and 100% the maximum.

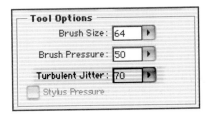

Using a similar example to that shown above, with all other settings constant, and with the mouse cursor depressed, but not moved, the effects of various Jitter values should be evident.

0% Jitter   50% Jitter   100% Jitter

Notice how in the first example, with no Jitter value applied, the pixels are moved in a fairly smooth manner, but as the Jitter values increase in the remaining two examples, the pixels are moved in an increasingly random order. As with the previous example, the end results you get when using various Jitter values will depend on your other settings, whether you click or click and drag, and also the resolution of the file with which you are working.

However you should find it useful for adding those wispy, irregular effects often needed when attempting to simulate natural media and paintings.

The Backdrop feature

In the previous version, use of the Liquify filter may have been limited because working with it was often a hit and miss situation. You never quite knew how the manipulated areas were changing from the original, or how they were interacting with other layers. Using the new **Backdrop** feature, you are now able to see how your manipulation differs from your original, how it interacts with existing layers, or both.

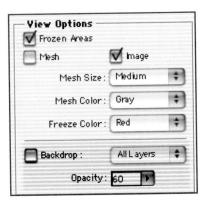

To illustrate how the backdrop option works, we'll create a very simple file and then choose various backdrop options.

Using the Backdrop feature

1. Open `spade.psd`, which can be downloaded from www.friendsofed.com, or create a similar file that has three layers, as indicated in the image:

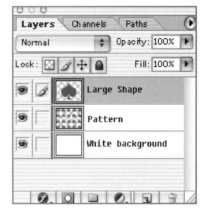

The bottom layer, called White background, is a solid layer filled with white.

2. Above it is a layer filled with a pattern with a transparent background, created from a spade vector shape. A noise filter has been applied to the pattern in an attempt to visually distinguish it from the other layer. The top layer is a large shape also created from the spade vector shape. All vector shapes have been rasterized.

3. Go to Filter > Liquify.

4. Deselect the Backdrop option so all you will see in the Liquify dialog box is the image contained on the current active layer, and the transparency checkerboard if the image was on a layer containing transparent areas. In the example shown, the active layer when the Liquify dialog box was launched is the Large Shape layer. Consequently the image in the Liquify preview with the Backdrop option deselected will appear thus:

All that is visible is the content of the target layer, and transparent areas are depicted by the usual checkerboard pattern.

To temporarily hide transparency, hold down the C key. As soon as the key is released, transparent areas will once again be represented by the checkerboard pattern.

5. If you wish to see the original large spade shape in conjunction with the modifications as you create them in the Liquify preview area, click the check box beside the Backdrop option, select the name of the layer – in this case Large Shape – from the drop down menu to the right, and then set an Opacity value for the visible Backdrop by either dragging the slider or entering a value in the Opacity field. Even if you set the Opacity for the backdrop at 100% it will never be as solid as the original image.

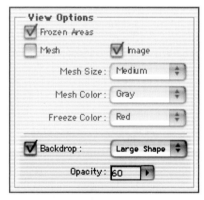

Note that the original, unmodified spade shape shows up as a fainter shape – this is the backdrop, and the modified shape is solid.

6. To see how the modified shape is interacting with a layer beneath or above it, target that particular layer in the drop down menu. In the example below, the Pattern layer has been chosen as the layer for the Backdrop.

7. Set the Backdrop layer choice to **All Layers**. Now a composite image is shown at the lower opacity, with your active layer shown at full strength as in the previous examples.

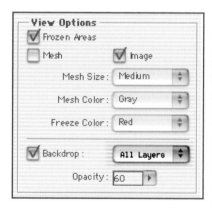
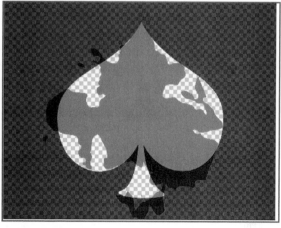

Note that on the odd occasion, dependent on your file components, layers, opacity values, and transparency, choosing the All Layers option may make it difficult for you to see what is happening. If this is the case, either deselect the Backdrop option, or target a specific layer according to your needs.

Saving and loading meshes

Whereas all the previous enhancements and new features to the Liquify filter introduced in this version may make have made working with this filter a little easier, the most powerful new feature affecting your workflow is the ability to save and then reload **Meshes**. The importance of this feature lies in a number of directions.

Using meshes means that you can speed up your work by applying the Liquify modifications to a low-resolution file, which can be considerably faster than working with your print-ready image. The mesh can then be saved, the high-resolution file loaded, and the mesh loaded and applied within seconds to that high-resolution file.

The second benefit associated with the ability to save meshes is that work does not have to be completed in one session. You can now begin working on a file and by saving the mesh, even if you choose not to apply the Liquify modifications to your image, and choose Cancel, you are able to reload the saved mesh at any stage and continue with your work.

Another advantage with saved meshes is that you can obviously load them and apply them to different images, or even create a number of meshes and apply them to the same image until you make your final choice. If you wanted to take this process one step further, you could write an action that applied a certain mesh to a series of files through the File > Automate > Batch command. This is a common requirement if you need to apply the same effect across a series of video screens.

To save a mesh, the process is as simple as saving a file. You create the mesh by applying various Liquify modifications to your image. The next step is to choose the **Save Mesh** option in the Liquify dialog box and navigate through your hard drive until you decide on a suitable folder in which to save the .msh file.

An optional step before you save the mesh is to actually view the mesh by checking the **Mesh** check box in the Liquify dialog box. Once you have saved the mesh, you can either click OK to apply the mesh to the image, or click Cancel.

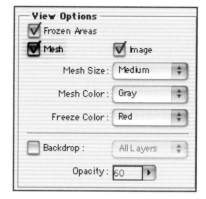

To load a saved mesh from within the Liquify dialog box, click on the **Load Mesh** button and then navigate through your hard drive to where the target .msh file is located.

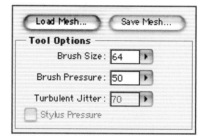

Once the file has been selected, the mesh will be instantly applied to the image. You can then choose whether to retain this mesh, or apply another mesh to the image by repeating the above steps.

Conclusion

The new tools and options for multiple undos and viewing backgrounds improve the functionality of the Liquify particular filter. The strongest and most effective feature regarding improved workflow is the ability to save, load, and re-use meshes.

Chapter 7

Vivid Light Blending Mode (Chapter 7)

Before

After

Linear Light Blending mode (Chapter 7)

Before

After

Pin Light Blending mode (Chapter 7)

Before

Base Layer

After

The Healing Brush tool (Chapter 8)

Before   After

The Patch tool (Chapter 8)

Before   After

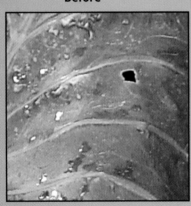 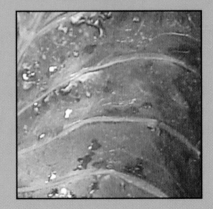

Using a pattern with the Patch tool (Chapter 8)

Before   After

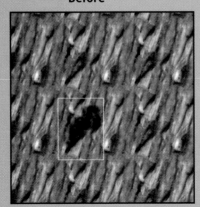 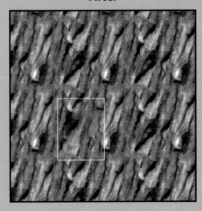

Selective optimisation for jpg (chapter 9)

Text at 250% zoom from the original image

Text at 250% zoom from jpg quality 40.

Image as jpg with maximum 65 and minimum 0 quality, using the text and shape   layers as masks.

Image as jpg with maximum 65 and minimum 0 quality, using the text and shape layers and the hats channel as masks.

Transparent web images (Chapter 9)

Dithered Transparency (Chapter 9)

Before

With dithering

Web Gallery (Chapter 12)

Layers Palette and Blending Mode Enhancements

What we'll cover in this chapter:

- *Understanding the new Layers palette layout*

- *Using Layer Opacity and Layer Fill correctly*

- *Trying out the new Blending Modes*

New layer elements

The new Layers palette has undergone a few cosmetic changes as well as some desirable functional improvements.

Locking layer elements

The first thing you may notice is the new 3D style buttons. These replace the icons at the foot of the palette and more noticeably replace the check boxes previously used for locking elements.

The Lock function works in exactly the same way as the previous version, but now you just have to click the icon instead of checking a box to enable the lock. The button will appear depressed. Clicking again releases the button and unlocks the required element.

Renaming layers

A welcome return from earlier versions is the ability to rename a layer simply by double-clicking the layer name. This replaces the previous cumbersome method of OPT/ALT + double-clicking.

Layer Fill option

This additional option gives you greater control over the normal layer Opacity option, which remains the same.

Reducing layer **Opacity** has the effect of reducing the image pixel opacity as well as any layer effects you have applied to it, such as a drop shadow. When reducing the layer **Fill** opacity, only the image pixel area is affected leaving any layer effects unchanged. The three examples that follow demonstrate how this looks in practice.

In this first picture, the flower is on a separate layer with a drop shadow layer effect applied. The layer Opacity is set to 100%.

Now, the flower picture layer has the layer Opacity reduced to 30%, but this also reduces the opacity of the drop shadow.

The Fill opacity is used in this example. The layer Opacity remains at 100%, but the Fill opacity has been reduced to 30%, reducing the actual image opacity, but leaving the drop shadow unaffected.

New Blending modes

Photoshop's existing collection of Blending modes now has five new additions (Linear Burn, Linear Dodge, Vivid Light, Linear Light, Pin Light). The underlying concept of Blending modes remains unchanged. What *has* changed in addition to the newcomers is the order in which the Blending modes are laid out. They now appear in a much more logical format being grouped by categories. For example, all the Blending modes that lighten an image appear in one group, as do all the Blending modes that darken an image.

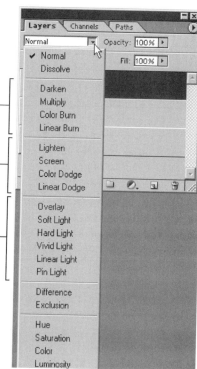

Most, but not all, Blending modes can be applied to paintbrushes as well as layers, as with previous versions.

Before we look at the new additions to the Blending modes, you may find a refresher helpful in respect of the terminology used to describe the components of the blend mode operation.

- Base color refers to the original color in the image or the bottom layer.

- Blend color refers to the color being applied or existing on the top layer.

- The result color is what you are left with after the blend has been performed.

Blending modes are accessed in the same way as in previous versions of Photoshop.

To demonstrate each of the new blend modes, the following two images were used. The spiral was used as the base color on the bottom layer and the flower was used as the blend color on the top layer.

Linear Burn

Linear Burn is the first of the new blend modes designed to darken images. Photoshop checks color information in each of the channels and reduces the brightness of the base color. The white element of the original flower picture is completely removed. Blending with white in Linear Burn mode has no effect on the underlying pixels, which is why we can see through to the spiral image.

The level of darkening is quite dramatic, but another characteristic of this mode is the way color is subdued. This is definitely not a mode to use for strong vibrant color effects. Where it does prove successful is in creating high contrast images, typical of a printmakers plate or linocut effects. The image below used the same flower image in the top layer and a medium blue mosaic pattern on the bottom layer. The photographic realism of the flower has been completely overshadowed resulting in a more illustrative piece of work.

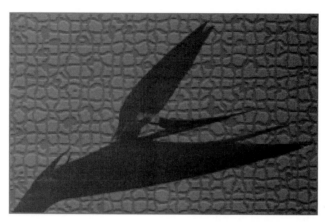

Once you know what the blend mode does, it is often helpful to ignore the descriptive name of the mode as this often suggests a much more limited range of uses.

Linear Dodge

This has the reverse effect of the Linear Burn in that reducing contrast lightens the base color. In this instance, black has no effect on the underlying pixels.

The image below uses three layers, the binoculars shape on the top layer, the lion on the middle, and the mosaic pattern on the bottom layer. Both the Binoculars and the Lion layers have had the Linear Dodge blend mode applied to them, resulting in the brightening effect being multiplied in the pixel area defined by the binoculars.

The binocular shape was filled with a dark gray color. Bearing in mind black has no effect and the dark gray color is only slightly lighter than black, the effect on the underlying pixels is quite subtle. The lighter the colors, the more radical is the effect on the underlying pixels.

Vivid Light

Vivid Light is a useful and highly creative addition to the Blending modes, as it is a combination of the Dodge and Burn modes. The decision on whether Dodge or Burn controls the result is based on the blend color (the color on the top layer). 50% gray is used as the deciding factor when Photoshop assesses the blend color. If the blend color is lighter than 50% gray, the underlying image is made lighter. Anything darker than 50% gray on the top layer and the underlying image is darkened.

In both cases the lightening or darkening effect is achieved through increasing or decreasing contrast.

A common characteristic of this blend mode is a flattening and simplifying of color. In many cases photographic images take on a hand painted look with a richness of color.

The fruit and vegetables image below was placed on the top layer and the bottom layer was filled with a medium blue color. The Vivid Light blend mode was then applied to the top layer resulting in the hand painted feel visible in the image on the right. The grayscale image you are looking at doesn't show the richness of color of course, but a flattening of color will be apparent when compared to the original. You can see the affect this has on the color images by looking at them in the color section of the book.

The Vivid Light blend mode is also very effective at adding impact color to what might be a very featureless image in terms of color. The flower image on the left is almost monochromatic. Placing a multi colored gradient layer below the flower layer and applying the Vivid Light blend mode to the flower layer instantly achieve a bold colorful effect.

Linear Light

There is a very subtle difference between Vivid Light and Linear Light. The principle remains the same between both modes. 50% gray is used to decide whether the underlying image is darkened or lightened, but where the Vivid Light mode uses an increase or decrease in contrast to cause the final effect, Linear Light increases or decreases the brightness.

The image to the right is the same white flower picture blended with the multi color gradient, but the blend mode used was Linear Light this time. The result is more subtle, as the effect has been produced by a change in brightness, rather than a change in contrast as with Vivid Light, the before and after color images can be seen in the color section.

Pin Light

The Pin Light blend mode is used to replace colors. Again it uses 50% gray as a deciding factor in how to change the underlying pixels. When the blend color is lighter than 50% gray (top layer) any pixels lighter than this on the base color (bottom layer) are not affected. Pixels on the base color layer darker than the blend color layer are then replaced.

The reverse is true when the blend color layer is darker than 50% gray. Now any pixels on the base color layer which are lighter then the blend color layer will be replaced, and pixels darker than the blend color layer will be unaffected.

The effect can result in quite startling color effects depending on the images used, though it does often have a destructive effect on the image and leaves more of an abstract piece of art, as in the picture opposite.

The following two pictures also use the Pin Light blend mode, not in a destructive manner but to change the colors so as to depict a different time phase. The palm tree was photographed in bright afternoon sunlight. This image was placed on the top layer and had the Pin Light blend mode applied. On the bottom layer was the right hand image, a pale cream to blue radial gradient.

The resulting image produces a simple, but effective simulation of moonlight. Again, these images can be seen in color in the color section.

Conclusion

The changes to the Layers palette may be fairly minor, but they are significant enough to move you a step closer to that ultimate streamlined workflow. The Blending modes, which on the surface appear to emulate their existing counterpart modes with a few extra tweaks, actually open up a whole new area of exploration. Once you have digested the technical process, the experimentation can really begin.

Chapter 8

Enhancing Your Images

What we'll cover in this chapter:

- *Introducing the Healing Brush tool*

- *Suggestions and tips for using the Healing Brush tool*

- *Using the Patch tool*

- *Hints and tips for using the Patch tool*

- *Enhanced image adjustment options*

- *The new Auto-Color command*

- *Enhanced auto correction options*

*For many Photoshop users, retouching and color correcting images forms a large part of their daily work. Any tools that are going to make that work easier, quicker, and more accurate have to be seen as valuable improvements in the application. The new **Healing** Brush, **Patch** tool, and the changes to the **Levels** dialog box and the **Auto-Color** command are such tools.*

Introducing the Healing Brush tool

The **Healing** Brush tool bears a strong resemblance to the Clone Stamp tool, but with some marked improvements in its ease of use. The Clone Stamp tool allowed you to subtly correct imperfections in images if you used it with extreme care, but all too often the results were not ideal. This is not to say that the Healing Brush tool is the answer to all your problems, but used effectively you will find it a vast improvement on the results often created with the Clone Stamp tool.

Where does the Healing Brush tool differ from the Clone Stamp tool? And why is it so much more powerful? At the simplest level, the Healing brush does the same as the Clone Stamp, with added benefits. Not only does it clone pixels from selected areas to cover up blemishes or imperfections, but also takes into consideration the tonality of the pixels in the area to be corrected.

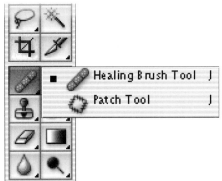

If you study the image below carefully, you'll notice how the blemishes in the Before image have been effortlessly removed in the After image using the Healing brush tool. This is not to suggest that the Healing Brush tool can only be used for correcting facial blemishes and wrinkles. You'll also find it extremely useful for removing scratches, dust, and other imperfections in aged photographs.

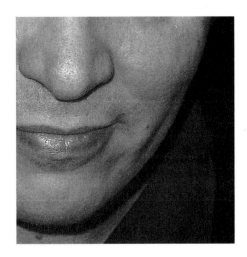
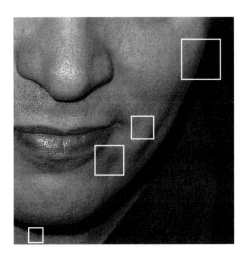

Before   After

A color example of using the Healing Brush tool can be seen in the color section of the book.

When would you use the Healing Brush tool?

Bearing in mind the apparent similarities between the Healing Brush tool and the Clone Stamp tool, it may be difficult at times to determine which tool to use. Unlike the Clone Stamp tool, the Healing Brush tool does not paint over the original image, but attempts to actually reconstruct the damaged area. If there is more damage than detail in the area to be healed, the original flaws may still be apparent. In such an instance you would probably get better results from using either the Clone Stamp tool or the **Patch** tool, which will be introduced later in this chapter.

Using the Healing Brush tool

Assuming a familiarity with the Clone Stamp tool, you'll find the options for using the new Healing Brush tool very similar. If you do not have a sample file to hand, the Old Image.jpg that is shipped with the application, located in the Sample files folder, should give you a chance to practice.

1. Select the Healing Brush tool (J) from the toolbox.

2. Choose a brush size and further brush options by clicking on the brush sample icon in the options bar and then setting additional options if required in the palette that appears.

Note that if you are using a digitizing tablet, you can use further options to vary the size of the Healing Brush tool by choosing an option from the Size drop down menu at the base of the palette.

- **Pen Pressure** – varies the size of the stroke in relation to the pressure being applied by the stylus.

- **Stylus Wheel** – uses the position of the stylus thumbnail as the basis of the stroke variation.

- **Off** – no variation is applied.

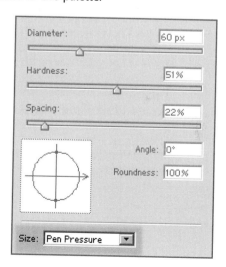

3. Choose a Blending mode from the drop down menu on the options bar.

Blending modes available are more limited than those available for the Clone Stamp tool, and include Normal, Multiply, Screen, Darken, Lighten, Color, Luminosity, and there is a new Blending mode available here – Replace.

Unlike the other modes, Replace does not actually heal the image, but concentrates on blending the noise component in the image. This limits the fading of film grain or other noise at the brush's edges that is often visible when the Clone Stamp tool is used with a soft brush. Use the Healing Brush tool in Replace mode – instead of the Clone Stamp Tool – if you need to correct a noisy image (for example one containing sand, hair, or film grain) with a smooth brush. With a hard brush, using the Healing Brush tool in Replace mode is the same as using the Clone Stamp Tool.

4. Choose a source that will be used for repairing the pixels from the Source options in the options bar. You can choose either a Sampled source from an image, or you can choose to use a Pattern, unless you are working with a 16-bit image, as they do not support the use of patterns.

If you choose the **Sampled** option, you will need to OPT/ALT+CLICK with the Healing Brush tool to select an area from which to sample the replacement pixels. You can sample from any area on an active layer within the image, but note that the Healing Brush tool only samples on a single layer – it does not create a merged sample from visible layers. You can also sample from a layer in another file in the same color mode, unless either the target or the destination file is in grayscale. As with the Clone Stamp tool, always try and sample from an area that is similar in color, tone, shade, and lighting to the area you wish to heal as this will make your attempts more successful.

If you elect to use a **Pattern** as you 'heal' the area, you'll need to check the Pattern option on the options bar as indicated, and then select a pattern from the Pattern drop down palette in the options bar.

5. Finally, select how you wish to align the sampled pixels. Once again, this feature has the same functionality as the Clone Stamp tool. With Aligned selected, the sampled pixels are applied continuously irrespective of whether you click and release the mouse. Whereas, if you deselect Aligned, you always start painting from that original sampled point whenever you continue painting.

6. Click and drag over the damaged area to blend the sampled and source pixels together and to remove the damage. Once again, as with the Clone Stamp tool, it is often a good idea to continuously resample as you paint. You will not notice the blending of the pixels while you are painting, the actual blend occurs each time you release the mouse.

Tips for working with the Healing Brush tool

-   The Healing Brush tool does not sample all layers, it only uses the active layer that was targeted when you OPT/ALT+click the source point for healing in the other document.

-   Unlike the Clone Stamp tool, you cannot paint onto an empty layer. This is because the Healing Brush tool draws information from the sample area and then blends it with the target area – the area you are painting. If you attempt to paint onto a blank layer, you are effectively blending the sampled area with a transparent area. Although you may see the paint being applied initially, it disappears once you release the mouse and Photoshop performs the blend calculations. If you really feel the need to safeguard your work, you can always copy the area to be repaired to another layer and then work on it there. Remember to copy slightly more than the area to be repaired so that the Healing Brush tool can interact with the adjacent pixels.

-   The Healing Brush tool does not have options for setting opacity as you paint. The following workarounds could be adopted quite efficiently:

    -   Use Edit > Fade Healing brush command (CMD/CTRL+SHIFT+F) to fade the effect after you have 'healed' an area.

    -   Apply the Healing Brush tool, take a Snapshot on the History palette, and then use the History brush to paint back in some of the healing at a lighter opacity.

- As previously mentioned, because the Healing Brush tool uses surrounding data for reconstruction, you may find that you have unwanted adjacent colors bleeding into the area you are repairing. To avoid this, it is often useful to make an accurate, hard-edged selection around the area you are trying to repair. Make the selection slightly bigger than the area you are trying to repair.

- As the Healing Brush tool uses the image data surrounding the defected area to do the reconstruction, you'll often find that you get better results if you use a hard-edged brush as opposed to a soft-edged brush.

- If the area you are trying to repair contains a lot of noise, such as film-grain, then you might find you get better results from a soft-edged brush.

Although the Healing Brush tool is a powerful new addition to the Photoshop arsenal of tools, you may find that it takes a little practice to get the results you want.

Introducing the Patch tool

The second of the new retouching tools introduced in this version is the **Patch** tool. Whereas the Healing Brush tool can be likened to the natural healing of a scar and if the damage is too great, the healing will not totally eliminate the scar; the Patch tool is similar to placing a patch over a damaged area. Like the Healing Brush tool, the Patch tool also takes the texture, lighting, and shading of the area into account.

Before

After

If you look at the leaf photograph above, you'll notice the hole in the leaf in the Before image. Whilst we could have used the Healing Brush tool to correct this, the damage to the area was fairly intense and it is likely that some of this damage would remain visible after the area had been healed. By using the Patch tool, an area near to the tear was selected and used as a sample area to blend with and correct the damaged area. You can also see a color example of this image in the color section of the book.

Using the Patch tool

There are a number of ways in which the Patch tool can be used, but each option starts with the concept of having a selection. The selection can be created using any of the traditional selection tools, or by using the Patch tool ⚙ in the same manner as you would the Lasso tool, by clicking and dragging to encompass an area. Furthermore, the familiar shortcuts of using SHIFT to add to a selection, or OPT/ALT to subtract from a selection work with the new Patch tool as well. Once you have made a selection, you can then either use a sample area of pixels or a pattern to patch the region.

Using a sample area of pixels – Method 1

1. Using either the Patch tool or a selection tool of your choice, click and drag to encompass the area in need of repair.

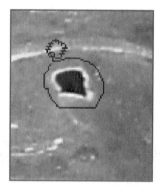

2. With the Patch tool as the active tool, select Source in the options bar.

3. Position the cursor within the selection outline, and drag the selection down to an area that will be used as a sample area to patch the damage. Release the mouse when the selection is over the desired pixels and the damaged area that was originally selected is patched with the pixels from the sample area.

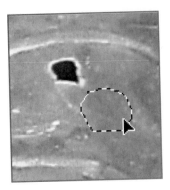 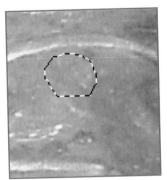

If you drag the selection to an area to use as your Patch sample and the result is not quite what you expected, you can continue to drag and reposition the selection outline over different areas until you are satisfied with how the sampled pixels have 'patched' the original damaged area.

Using a sample area of pixels – Method 2

Similar in process to the first method, this approach selects the area to be used to patch the repaired section first.

1. With the Patch tool or any other selection tool, click and drag to select the undamaged area which will be used as the sample pixels.

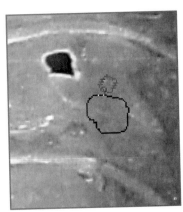

2. With the Patch tool as the active tool, select Destination in the options bar.

3. Position the cursor within the selection outline, and then drag the selection over the damaged area. Release the mouse and the damaged area is patched with the pixels from the sample area.

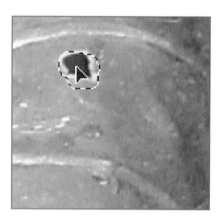
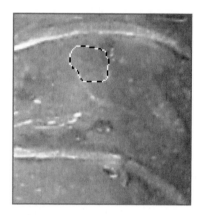

Using a pattern to fill the damaged area

In addition to using pixels sampled from the image to patch damaged areas, you can also fill the damaged area with a pattern.

1. As before, use either the Patch tool or a selection tool to select the area to be patched.

2. Ensure that the Patch tool is active. Select a pattern from the Pattern drop down palette in the options bar, and click Use Pattern.

The selected area will be filled with the pattern chosen from the options bar.

 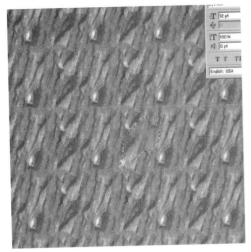

Tips for working with the Patch tool

- If you wish to create a feathered selection, you can make the selection using the Patch tool and then go to Select > Feather. You cannot set a feather value before you create the selection as with other tools.

- As with the Healing Brush tool, the Patch tool has no options for setting the opacity of the patch. You may wish to use these workarounds to control the strength of the Patch:

  - Use the Edit > Fade Patch Selection command (CMD/CTRL+SHIFT+F) to fade the effect after you have 'patched' an area; or,

  - Apply the Patch tool, take a Snapshot on the History palette, and then use the History brush to paint back in some of the patch at a lighter opacity.

- When patching using pixels sampled from the image, selecting small areas will give you better results. Being precise about those selections means that you are less likely to include undesired pixels in either your source or destination pixel selections.

- As all edits take place on the original target layer and not on a blank layer, you may wish to duplicate the area to be patched and the sample area to another layer before patching.

- It is sometimes difficult to see the effects of the patch when the selection edges are visible. You may have a better perspective if you hide the edges when looking at the results of the patch.

Like the Healing Brush tool, the Patch tool, when used with care, will make that problem of retouching damaged images easier.

Enhanced image adjustment controls

Enhancements to the color correction tools in version 7 include the new **Auto Color** command and improved auto correction options in the Levels dialog box.

The Auto Color command

In addition to the previous auto commands for Levels and Contrast, the new Auto Color command improves images with a color cast by adjusting both the contrast and color in the image. As with all of the auto commands, it should be used with care as using the manual Levels or Curves controls often attain better results. Having said that, the feature does seem to work effectively on images.

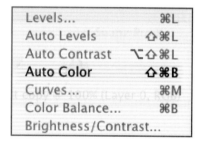

When you invoke the Auto Color command by choosing Image > Adjustments > Auto Color (CMD/CTRL+SHIFT+B), the midtones are assigned more neutral values, and shadow and highlight pixels are clipped based on the values set in the **Auto Corrections** dialog box. These values will be discussed in more detail in the next section of this chapter. Unlike the Auto Levels command which clips each channel independently to increase the tonal range of the image, Auto Color looks for the average darkest and lightest pixels in the image, and uses them as the shadow and highlight values. Additionally it adjusts the midtones in the image so that those colors that are close to a neutral value are changed to the target midtone color.

In assessing the accuracy of this feature, it is essential that you actually apply it to an image with an incorrect color balance. If you have a digital camera at your disposal, you can easily create some of these images by changing the white balance to an incorrect setting and taking some new images. Failing that, the Peppers.jpg file located in the Samples folder within the Photoshop application is a good sample image to use.

Using the Auto Color command

To effectively note how the Auto Color command removes the color cast, you may wish to follow this tutorial.

1.   Open the file called `Peppers.jpg` from the Samples folder.

2.   Using the **Color Sampler** tool, place some sample points in the midtone area of the background as indicated in the screenshot. Note the values on the Info palette. You may notice that this particular image has a distinctly yellow-green cast in the midtones – particularly evident in that background area.

3.   Create an additional three copies of the file using the Image > Duplicate command. Name the first copy Auto Contrast, the second, Auto Levels, and the third, Auto Color.

4.   Adjust each of the images using the Adjustments command, which correlates to the file's name.

5.   Tile all four images – the original untouched `Peppers.jpg`; and the three duplicate files. Notice how the Auto Contrast command has had the least effect on the color cast in the image. This is as expected because the feature makes highlights appear lighter and shadows darker, without affecting color.

Auto Levels has made a better job of handling the color cast, although if you study the color values in the Info palette, there is still a strong yellow cast in the midtones.

In the final image, the one to which you applied the Auto Color command, the cast in the background has been neutralized; and the color of the bowl is far more balanced.

6.   Save the files for use a little later in the chapter.

Note that the Auto Color command is an RGB tool. It is not available if your file is in any other color mode.

Expanded Auto Correction Options

Although you could set options from within the Levels and Curves dialog box in previous versions of Photoshop, they were limited to setting the clipping values used for the highlights and shadows when you chose the Auto option. Added to that, access to the Options screen only became visible when the OPT/ALT key was depressed within either the Curves or Levels dialog box. That button is now directly visible in either of the above-mentioned features.

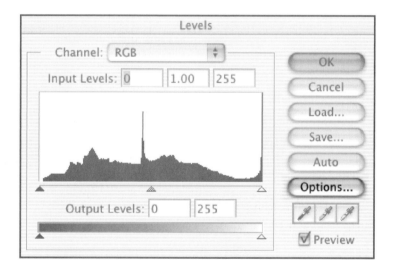

By accessing the Auto Correction Options dialog box, you can specify how the tonal range of the image will be affected when you select Auto within either the Levels or Curves dialog box. Additionally, you can set color values for the shadows, midtones, and highlights; and specify clipping values for the shadows and highlights.

These values can be set just for that particular episode or you can save the settings as default settings so that they are used when you use Curves or Levels, and when you use any of the three Auto commands from the Adjustments sub-menu.

Choosing an algorithm option

To display the Auto Corrections dialog box, open either the Levels (CMD/CTRL+L) or Curves (CMD/CTRL+M) dialog box; and click on the Options button located at the lower right of the dialog box.

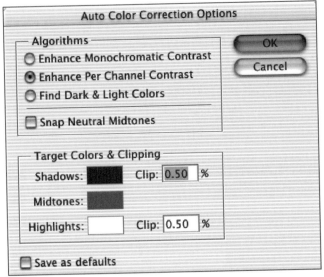

The section headed Algorithms determines how using the Auto option within the Curves or Levels dialog box will affect the tonal range within the image.

- **Enhance Monochromatic Contrast** – this algorithm will give you a result similar to using the Auto Contrast command. It works by clipping all channels within the image identically, and makes no attempt to alter the color balance.

- **Enhance Per Channel Contrast** – this is the algorithm used by the Auto Levels command. Unlike Enhance Monochromatic Contrast, this command clips the color channels independently, consequently increasing the tonal range in each channel. Using this command may remove color casts, but conversely it may also introduce color casts into the image.

- **Find Dark & Light Colors** – this is the algorithm used by the Auto Color command where the average of the darkest and lightest pixels in the image are used as the values for the shadow and highlight.

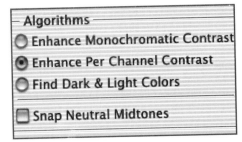

Eliminating color casts in the midtones

The **Snap Neutral Midtones** option is used to neutralize color casts in the midtone areas of an image. It works by adjusting the midtones so that those colors that are close to a neutral value are changed to the target midtone color. The target midtone color is either set in the lower part of the Options dialog box; or from the main Curves or Levels dialog box it is accessed by double-clicking on the midtone eyedropper. This feature is used by the Auto Color command.

☐ **Snap Neutral Midtones**

Choosing different algorithm settings

To give you a practical example of how the three settings affect the tonal range of the image, open the Peppers.jpg file located in the Photoshop Samples folder, along with the three files you created in the earlier exercise in the Auto Color section of this chapter.

1. Tile all the files, bearing in mind that you will be opening either the Curves or Levels dialog box, and the Options dialog box within that; and you will want to see as much of all four images as possible.

2. Select the original Peppers.jpg; and choose Options from within either the Curves or Levels dialog box.

3. Select each of the algorithm options and notice how when you select:

    ◼ Enhance Monochromatic Contrast – the image is similar in appearance to the file called Auto Contrast.

    ◼ Enhance Per Channel Contrast – the file looks like the Auto Levels file.

    ◼ Find Dark and Light Colors – alters the image so that it bears a similarity to the Auto Color image. However, if you look very closely at the midtone area where the original color samplers were placed, there is still a color cast. Granted it is not as strong as the one that remained when you either chose the Auto Level menu command or when you selected the Enhance Per Channel Contrast algorithm. This is because the midtones have not yet been affected.

4. With the Dark and Light Color algorithm selected, check the Snap Neutral Midtones box; and notice how the color cast in the midtones is removed.

Setting the target color values and clipping levels

In the lower area of the dialog box, you'll notice an area headed **Target Colors & Clipping**. Although these concepts are not actually new to Photoshop, having these options here enables you to set values each time you adjust an image. You can also set the values as defaults for use whenever you use the Curves or Levels command, or any of the auto correction menu commands.

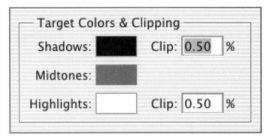

Clicking on the color swatches next to Shadows, Midtones, or Highlights will display the Color Picker dialog box, similar to what happens when you double-click on any of the eyedroppers in the Curves and Levels dialog box. However, dependent on whether you wish to save these target values as defaults, or merely use them for one particular image is an additional option here.

To the right of the Shadows and Highlights color swatches are two fields for setting the clipping values. To specify how much to clip black and white pixels, enter percentages in the Clip text boxes. A value between 0.5% and 1% is recommended, although sometimes better results can be attained using a slightly lower clipping percentage.

By clipping, or ignoring, a certain percentage of the lightest and darkest pixels in an image, you can be more confident that the adjustments made are based on a better representation of the pixels as it has ignored the extremely light or dark pixels.

If you wish to save new settings, including all options in this dialog box as the default values, select Save as Default. This means that any options selected will be applied automatically each time you click the Auto button with the Curves or Levels dialog box. Additionally the target color values and the clipping rate set will be applied each time you use any of the Auto correction options from the Adjustments submenu.

Conclusion

With these improvements to the auto correction options, including the addition of the new Auto Color command, the process of creating that perfectly balanced image has become a lot quicker and more accurate. Plus, the new image correction tools – the Healing Brush tool and the Patch tool – make correcting an image all that much smoother.

Chapter 9

Optimizing and Exporting Images

What we'll cover in this chapter:

- *Selective optimization techniques for jpg images*

- *Selective optimization techniques for gif images*

- *Optimizing techniques in ImageReady*

- *New techniques for mapping colors to transparency*

- *Creating dithered transparency*

- *Creating WBMP images for cell phones, PDAs, and other hand held devices.*

- *Creatively controlling images prior to WBMP conversion*

Optimizing web images

One of Photoshop's greatest strengths in recent years has been its ability to ease the arduous task of optimizing images for the web. Optimization itself has become a true art as designers work to achieve that fine balance between acceptable file size and good visual quality. For the majority of Internet users worldwide, broadband Internet connection is still the preserve of a small band of users, so the need to maintain respectable file size is as vital as ever.

Photoshop 7.0, and its counterpart, ImageReady 7.0, have addressed this situation by offering even greater flexibility and control in determining what levels of compression should be used on any given part of an image.

In case you are wondering what happened to ImageReady versions 4, 5, and 6, don't worry – you haven't missed anything. ImageReady has made the gargantuan leap from version 3 to 7 in one step to bring it in line with Photoshop 7.

Selective optimization for jpg

In a perfect Internet world, all photographic or continuous tone type images would be compressed using the jpg format. All flat color type images would use gif compression. This accepted formula works fine until you need to combine photographic images with vector artwork or text. Vector artwork and text always suffer visually when jpg compression is used at modest levels of compression. Decreasing the amount of compression can improve matters visually, but the file size grows to unacceptable levels. This undesirable scenario holds true if you were to use gif compression instead. While the text and vector shapes would look good, the photographic element of the image would suffer both visually and with increased file size.

Photoshop 7 provides a way round this problem by allowing you to apply different levels of compression to selected areas of the image. For example, an image such as the one described above where text and a vector logo are placed on top of a photograph could use the jpg format, but low levels of compression could be applied to the text and logo, thereby preserving as much quality as possible. Higher levels of compression could be applied to the photographic areas where the jpg lossiness would not be so noticeable.

Although this has been possible in earlier versions, the techniques that can be used to accomplish it have been improved. The secret is in masking elements. This is not entirely new to Photoshop 7 as it was possible to use channels as masks in previous versions of the Save for Web operation. Photoshop 7 provides a compact dialog box that allows you to nominate a vector shape layer, a text layer, and/or a channel to use as a mask.

Let's put the new techniques through their paces by seeing how they work with a difficult image similar to the one I have described. If you want to download the image and try out the settings for yourself it is available from www.friendsofed.com, and called `TravelAsia.psd`.

This file consists of the photo on the bottom layer, a vector shape layer housing the flame logo, and a text layer for the phrase "TravelASIA".

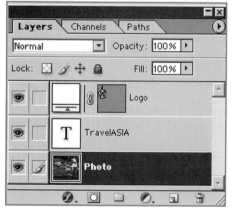

The challenge is to keep the text and logo as crisp as possible while preserving the photographic qualities of the boat image, and keeping the file size respectable. Because the majority of the image is photographic, jpg compression is the format of choice.

Go to File > Save For Web.

The Save for Web dialog box shows no obvious changes from earlier versions.

For this kind of photographic image, a jpg quality setting of about 40 would provide acceptable image quality and file size. However it is the text and logo that create a problem in this case.

This picture shows a section from the image with a quality setting of 40, zoomed in at 250%. Although the photographic elements still look acceptable, the text shows the tell tale signs of lossy compression. What was clean, flat color is now corrupted with digital artifacts, a side effect of jpg compression. The logo suffered a similar fate.

To improve the visually quality of the text it was necessary to increase the quality level to 65. The picture below shows the text at this increased quality level.

While this has improved the text and logo, it has had little effect on the quality of the photographic elements, which looked fine anyway. The file size has ballooned from 35 K to 62 K at the current quality level – almost twice the file size just to sharpen the text.

To remedy this situation we are going to use the new options to define where the quality should be emphasized. We'll do this by making use of the new dialog box to nominate our text and logo to be used as masks.

In the Save for Web dialog box click the small button next to the quality setting drop down.

This opens the **Modify Quality Setting** dialog box.

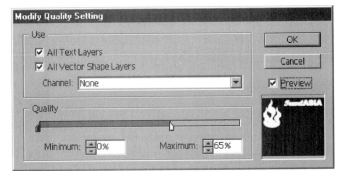

Selecting the check boxes labeled **All Text Layers** and **All Vector Shape Layers** will create a mask based on the elements on those layers. The thumbnail preview in the bottom right of the dialog box displays the text and logo elements as white, and all other areas as black. (Note that if you have rasterized text or shape layers, they will not show up as white and cannot be used for masking.)

To specify the quality setting for the white areas use any of the following methods:

- Drag the *white* marker on the **Quality** slider to the right to increase or to the left to decrease.

- Type a number in the **Maximum** numeric field to a maximum of 100.

- Click the up and down arrows next to the numeric field.

To specify the quality setting for the black areas use any of the following methods:

- Drag the *black* marker on the **Quality** slider to the right to increase or to the left to decrease.

- Type a number in the **Minimum** numeric field to a maximum of 100.

- Click the up and down arrows next to the numeric field.

Note that the Minimum setting cannot be higher than the Maximum setting, although they can hold identical values. If you did apply identical values to the Minimum and Maximum settings, both the black and white areas would have the same quality setting applied, which of course defeats the object of this operation.

The picture here is the finished result with the Maximum set to 65, which achieves the objective of acceptable quality text and logos. This image now weighs in at 55 K, 7 K less than the 62 K we were left with when we used the same quality setting prior to using the masks. A saving of over 11% is highly significant with regard to our overloaded telephone lines.

So where is the downside? Take a look at the hats and top of the woman's shoulders. They now look pixelated because they have the highest amount of compression applied to them. I left the Minimum set to 0%. The Minimum setting applies to all the black areas as seen in the thumbnail preview. The hats have suffered far more than the rest of the photographic elements.

Creating a mask from an alpha channel

To resolve this we need to make a selection of the hats and save the selection as an alpha channel called Hats. (As well as creating masks from vector shape layers and text layers, Photoshop 7 is able to do the same with an alpha channel.)

In order to do this, we need to cancel the saving operation to return to Photoshop's normal workspace. As we don't want to lose the modifications we have made so far, select Save Settings from the context menu, and save the settings as `TravelAsia.irs`.

Once you have saved the required selection, return to the Save for Web dialog, and click on TravelAsia from the settings drop-down. Then, in the Modify Quality Setting dialog box, select the desired channel from the drop down box.

A new mask is added and the preview becomes updated, now showing the text, flame logo, and hats as white elements.

Here is a section of the newly optimized image showing the hats with their improved quality based on a setting of 65, the same as the text and logo.

How about the file size? It grew by 14 bytes, which in the context of time roughly translates to the blink of an eye.

If large areas of the image that are not being controlled by masks have suffered too greatly (the black areas as defined in the thumbnail preview) you can use the **Minimum** slider to increase quality in those areas, but beware, the file size will start to creep up and soon you will be back where you started before the masks were introduced.

Selective optimization for gif

The same principle applies when converting images to gif format.

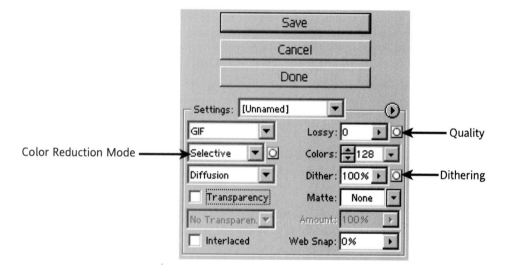

There are now three options where text layers, vector shape layers, and alpha channels can be used as a mask and quality and file size can be adjusted selectively. In each case clicking the small button next to the drop down box displays the Modify Quality Setting dialog box. The three options are labeled in the diagram above and will appear whenever the gif setting is selected.

- **Color Reduction Mode** – select the predefined color palette to generate the color table or use your own customized table. When using the mask to modify the color settings, white areas of the mask will be accorded the most importance, and so their colors will change the least.

- **Lossy** – define the amount of lossiness to be applied to the image. The highest level of quality is defined by the minimum value, with 0% being the uppermost.

- **Dithering** – when Diffusion is specified, the amount of Dither can be set ranging from 0% to 100%. White areas of the mask are given the most dithering.

None of these options are completely new to version 7 and function in exactly the same way as in previous versions. The only new elements are the ability to use a mask to modify the color settings, and the fact that vector shape layers and text layers can be used as masks.

Selective optimizing in ImageReady

ImageReady offers this function in the same way as Photoshop, although there is no Save for Web option. Everything appears in the main window. This can make it a better choice for the optimization process. If you need to create channels from selections to add to your mask, you can work with the image in place, rather than having to leave a dialog box and save or lose your settings.

The **Optimize** palette provides access to the same settings as in the Photoshop Save for Web dialog box.

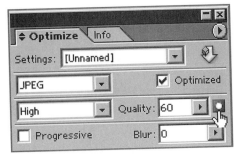

Whether you are in Photoshop or ImageReady, png-8 format is also available to use with masks and functions in exactly the same way.

Creating transparent web images

The gif 89a is the most commonly used format for creating web images with transparent areas. The process of creating transparent images has become increasingly streamlined in recent upgrades of Photoshop but the current process has to be the simplest and most efficient yet.

The most popular scenario for using transparent images is when circular or irregular shaped images, such as buttons and logos, need to be placed on a browser background color that differs from the original image background color. As the process has become so simple, it opens the door to a wide variety of new creative uses.

This logo has been designed so that the letter T can be made transparent. The logo can then be placed in a web page on top of a background image, a table background image, or within a layer using DHTML. If you wish to experiment with the file, it can be downloaded from www.friendsofed.com, and is called `Travelguides.psd`.

The image is a layered file. Go to File > Save for Web. In the Save for Web dialog box the color or colors you wish to become transparent need to be selected. This can be done in either of the following ways:

- Use the eyedropper to select the color in the preview window.

- Click the color swatch in the color table. Selected colors are highlighted with a black rectangle.

If you want to select more than one color, the SHIFT and CMD/CTRL keys work as modifiers here.

Next, either click the **Transparency** button to map all selected colors to transparency, or click the context menu button from the color table and select Map/Unmap Selected Colors to/from Transparent.

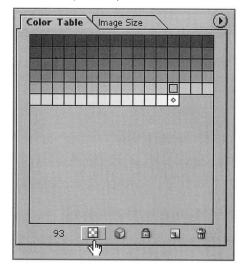

The selected color(s) becomes transparent immediately in the preview window.

The newly created transparent color appears in the color table in two halves, divided diagonally. The top half shows the former color and the bottom half shows the transparent gray/white check.

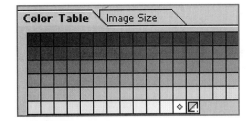

The finished transparent gif image can now be used multiple times over different photographic images in web pages without any further editing in Photoshop. You can see an example of the finished image in the color section of the book.

Returning a transparent color to its original opaque color

To reverse transparency, select the color or colors that you made transparent in the color table, and then either click the Transparency button or select Map/Unmap Selected Colors to/from Transparent from the context menu.

Returning all transparent colors to opaque without selecting first

Click the context menu button from the color table and select Unmap All Transparent Colors.

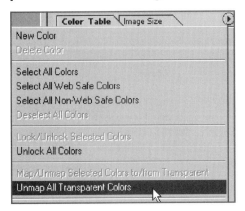

Creating dithered transparency images

Why would you need to create a dithered transparency? The most common reason is when you want to create a drop shadow effect on your artwork and position the artwork over a multi-colored or photographic background.

In the case of single color backgrounds the solution is simple. You can nominate a matte color to match the color of the browser background. This has been the standard Photoshop process for some time but it is limited. Firstly, it only works with single color backgrounds, and secondly if you want to use the graphic multiple times on different colored backgrounds you have to edit the graphic for every different color.

The problem lies in the fact that the gif format supports transparency, as we have seen, but not partial transparency. So shadows and similar effects are not possible. The pixel must be completely transparent or completely opaque, but no half measures in between.

Photoshop 7 strives to overcome this problem by mixing opaque and transparent pixels in a dithered pattern, creating the illusion of semi transparency.

Let's work through an example of the process. The gif image we are going to use is a butterfly with a drop shadow effect. This is called `butterfly.psd` and can be downloaded form www.friendsofed.com. On a plain white background the shadow looks subtle and convincing, as it would with any plain color background.

This flower picture is the image that will be used as its background in the web browser. To make it even more difficult, we shall assume there are dozens of different flower pictures that will be used on different pages throughout the web site, all requiring the butterfly logo to be placed on top.

This picture shows an attempt at creating our required design by saving the butterfly as a conventional transparent gif and placing it over the flower photo background in a web page.

Clearly the result is very poor, but serves to highlight the limitation of the transparent gif format.

Let's run through the process of dithering the transparency to improve the image.

Dithering transparency

1. In the original butterfly image I hid the background layer so just the butterfly artwork and its drop shadow sub-layer were visible. Alternatively the background layer could have been deleted altogether.

2. Next go to the File menu and then Save for Web.

3. In the Save for Web dialog box, select the gif format and amount of colors you want to use as you would normally for a gif.

4. Make sure the **Transparency** check box is checked, then click the drop down box below it.

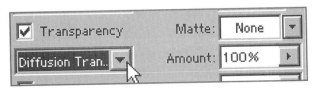

5. Four options are offered in this drop down box:

- **No Transparency Dither**: Creates a normal transparent image without dithering.

- **Diffusion Transparency Dither**: Creates a dithered pattern on partially transparent pixels. Diffusion of the dithered effect is produced across adjacent pixels.

- **Pattern Transparency Dither**: Partially transparent pixels receive a halftone pattern effect emulating traditional printing methods.

- **Noise Transparency Dither**: This effect is closest to the diffusion option, except the pattern is not diffused across adjacent pixels. The concept is similar to when you apply a noise filter to a gradient to break up the regularity, resulting in no obvious seams.

If you opt for the Diffusion Transparency Dither, the percentage amount field becomes enabled. Higher values result in greater degrees of diffusion.

Here's the finished result viewed in a web browser with the transparent dithered butterfly image placed over the flower image. The Diffusion Transparency Dither option setting was used with the amount set to 100%. Because the butterfly is an independent image with its own dithered transparency, it can be used multiple times over any background, including photos, gradients, patterns, and multi-colored images.

You don't have to be highly discerning to notice that the result is still not as good as the effect you would achieve in Photoshop, but it is another option at your disposal (the before and after color images can be seen in the color section). As with all digital design issues there are many ways to arrive at a solution. Ultimately it comes down to personal preference and available time. What we are dealing with here is not any shortcoming of Photoshop, but the limitations of current Web browsers and file format compatibility.

Creating images in WBMP format

The increased use of hand held devices such as cell phones and PDA's has generated a need for an optimized graphic format capable of delivering images to this new growing audience. That format has now been standardized as WBMP (Wireless Bitmap) and is fully supported by Photoshop and ImageReady 7.0.

The WBMP format is a 1-bit color format, supporting only black and white pixels. On the face of it, creating an image with just black and white pixels may not seem to be worth the effort, but a surprisingly large range of imagery is possible with Photoshop's help. Think about the result when using the Threshold filter, which reduces the image to black and white pixels and yet produces some very stylized effects.

This photograph is one of Photoshop's sample images.

Let's see what we can accomplish with the WBMP format. All the options for WBMP are accessed from File > Save for Web in Photoshop 7 or from the **Optimize** palette in ImageReady 7.0.

The image shows the Optimize palette in ImageReady with WBMP selected from the format drop down box. As with Dithered Transparency, there are four options defining the final style of the image. These are available from the lower drop down box as pictured.

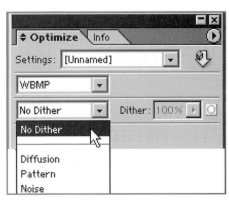

Selecting **No Dither** produces a simple black and white image with no further options.

The other three options produce the same results as with Dithered Transparency and are summarized again below.

- **Diffusion** – creates a dithered pattern on partially transparent pixels. Diffusion of the dithered effect is produced across adjacent pixels.

- **Pattern** – partially transparent pixels receive a halftone pattern effect.

- **Noise** – similar to the diffusion option, except that the pattern is not diffused across adjacent pixels and so the likelihood of obvious seams appearing is reduced.

Opting for **Diffusion** enables the percentage amount field, where the amount of diffusion can be controlled.

The image below on the left was set to 100% Diffusion resulting in the closest to a photographic image. The right-hand image was set to 50% Diffusion. The amount of diffusion has no impact on the final file size. The decision on which option to use is really down to personal preference and whether a more photographic or logo style effect is desired.

At the start of this chapter we looked at selective optimization where you could automatically generate a mask from a text layer, a vector shape layer, or an alpha channel. The same options are available to you when creating a WBMP image. Click the button next to the Dither box to display the options as before.

Fine tuning images for WBMP conversion

One drawback of using the No Dither option is that you have no control over which pixels are converted to black and which are converted to white. The Diffusion option does give you more control as you can see from the above examples, but you may prefer not to have a dithered image.

One way around this is to prepare the image prior to converting to WBMP by creating a 1-bit color image where you control, to a certain extent, the range of black and white pixels, using the Threshold filter, as I mentioned earlier.

Go to Image > Adjustments > Threshold.

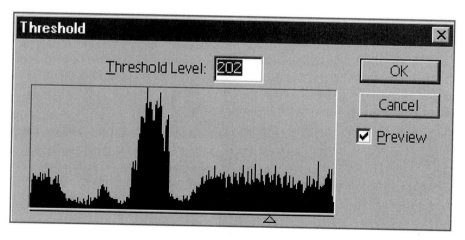

The Threshold command will convert a color or grayscale image to a black and white image. The Threshold Level is determined by the slider in the dialog box below the histogram. This histogram shows the luminance level of the pixels in the image. Drag the slider to the right to increase the amount of black pixels and drag to the left to increase the amount of white pixels.

Typically the Threshold command is used when assessing the lightest and darkest areas in an image, but it is great for adjusting an image to prepare it for WBMP format.

Using a Threshold level of 202 retains a little of the texture of the feathers on the bird's head.

To make the feathers stand out as black requires a darkening of the whole image, which also disposes of the detail of the eye, which isn't desirable.

Let's undo the Threshold command, and make a selection of the eye. Invert the selection and apply a Threshold level of 202 again.

Now invert the selection again and apply the Threshold command once more at a level of 38. This now only affects the eye area and allows you to control the amount of detail in the eye. The finished result appears here:

Now it's a simple case of saving the image in WBMP format with no dither.

Conclusion

Technology with regard to the web or any form of digital images is going to continue to forge ahead at a frenetic pace in the coming years. The challenge of creating high quality, low file size images remains at the forefront of design software development.

The optimization techniques in this latest release of Photoshop and ImageReady provide you with the tools to work creatively and efficiently in what has become a demanding and highly competitive environment.

Chapter 10

Creating Rollovers in ImageReady

What we'll cover in this chapter:

- Introduction to the new Rollovers palette

- Creating a navigation bar with JavaScript rollovers

- Editing mouse actions

- Previewing live effects

- Creating and applying rollover styles

- Creating animated rollovers

- Unifying states across rollovers

It is difficult to find a web page today without the ubiquitous rollover button image appearing somewhere within it. As an instrument for user feedback it plays a vital role in interface design and has become almost as standard as the hyperlink itself.

ImageReady has enabled the designer to incorporate rollover images into their page design for some time without the need to write or understand the JavaScript language that makes the rollover possible. Although this has been a great boon to designers and non-programmers, the implementation of rollovers in ImageReady hasn't been as clean cut as it might have been. The problem was that all the different states could not be viewed simultaneously. As well as slowing down workflow, it made it very easy to make errors by applying effects to the wrong layers.

In ImageReady 7.0 this has all changed, with the introduction of the new **Rollovers** palette. This allows you to control all rollover states, as well as gif animations and image maps, in a single palette. You can then make changes simply by clicking, in the Rollovers palette, on the state you want to amend, and applying the required effect.

Creating a navigation bar with rollovers

The original artwork for this navigation bar was created in Photoshop in exactly the way you would have expected. If you would like to use our file to work through creating rollovers, it is called `rollover.psd` and is available for download at www.friendsofed.com.

Each element was created on its own layer.

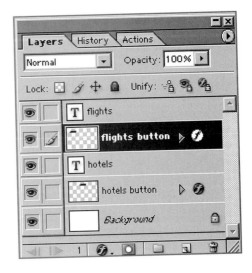

1. From the Layers palette, select the layer containing the artwork that you want to be the rollover. In this case it was the layer called flights button.

2. If you cannot see the Rollovers palette on the screen, go to Window > Rollovers.

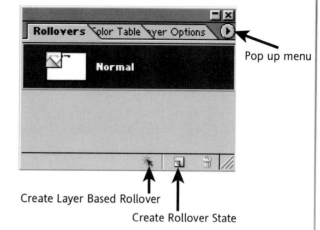

Pop up menu

Create Layer Based Rollover

Create Rollover State

The Rollovers palette closely resembles the Layers palette. The standard "layer" that appears by default is called Normal. This represents all the artwork on all the layers in your file.

3. Click the **Create layer-based rollover** icon as shown above.

Clicking this icon generates a slice based on the artwork in the selected layer in the Layers palette. It also creates a new state in the Rollovers palette.

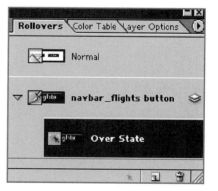

Slice is the term used for the first layer created, and **State** is used for all the following sub-layers.

The slice is automatically named "navbar_flights button". This name derives from the file name that had been saved previously, and the name of the layer on which the slice is based. It refers to the artwork in its initial state, in other words, the button as the user first sees it on the web page and before they click or roll over it.

The next state is named "Over State" and refers to what the user will see as they move their mouse over the button. At the moment, the initial state and rollover state are the same, so the next thing to do is to apply a change to the artwork for the Over State.

4. Make sure Over State is selected in the Rollovers palette. In the Layers palette, making sure the flights button layer is still selected, click the **Add a layer style** icon at the bottom of the Layers palette and select **Color Overlay**.

5. From the Color Overlay palette that appears, select your chosen color from the drop down box.

6. The Rollovers palette is on the same palette set as the Color Overlay. Click the Rollovers tab that is visible on the left of the palette as in the picture above.

You will now see that the button in the rollover state layer has changed color to reflect your choice. The initial slice remains unchanged.

If you only want an Over State, that's all you have to do, but let's create a second state. This second state will mean that the button will change when the user clicks on it and the mouse button is depressed.

7. Click the **Create rollover state** icon.

A second state appears named "Down State".

The Down State artwork is, at the moment, the same color and effect as the Over State, so we need to change it. The process is the same as before, but this time let's apply an effect rather than a color.

8. Make sure Down State in the Rollovers palette is selected, and then click the Add a layer style icon at the bottom of the Layers palette and select **Bevel and Emboss**.

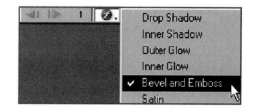

The Bevel and Emboss palette now appears.

9. To create the illusion of the button being pressed in, I clicked the Down radio button and left all the other settings as the default. Click back on the Rollovers tab to see the palette become updated with your latest editing.

Clicking each of the states in the Rollovers palette will allow you to see the artwork referring to each state, but it is also possible to preview the working rollover whilst still in ImageReady.

Previewing rollover effects

Click the **Preview Document** icon in the main toolbox or use the keyboard shortcut – Y.

You can now place the cursor over the button and click to see the Over and Down states in action.

Once you are in preview mode you will be prevented from carrying out other functions, so when you have finished previewing either press Y, the Esc key, or click the **Cancel preview** icon towards the top right of the screen to return to normal editing mode.

Creating a Selected state

Good interface design dictates that the user should always know where they are within the site at any time. The simplest and most effective way to do this is to dim the button of the current page. This is known as the **Selected** state. This state can be incorporated into the rollover button, removing the need to create additional graphics.

1. In the Rollovers palette, select the Down State, and then click the Create rollover state icon.

A new state is created, called "Selected State", based on the previously selected Down State showing the "pressed in" button. To signify this is the current page let's change the color to a darker shade.

2. Click the Add a layer style icon at the bottom of the Layers palette as you did previously, and select Color Overlay. Choose a darker shade and click back on the Rollovers tab to see the complete rollover updated with all its different states.

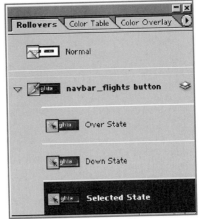

Previewing the rollover and clicking the flights button will cause the Selected State to stay active signifying you are in the flights page. This state will remain active until another rollover is selected.

Changing rollover states

When you create new states, ImageReady automatically allocates the type of state in a logical sequence based on the order in which the user would use a button. The mouse action, known as an Event in JavaScript coding, describes how the mouse interacts with the graphic. For example, Over (when the mouse cursor is over the graphic) is followed by Down (when the mouse button is pressed down and the cursor is over the graphic) which is followed by Selected (when the mouse button has been pressed and released). However you are able to change these states depending on the effect you wish to achieve.

There are a number of ways to change the mouse action within each state (For this example we shall assume you want to change the Down State from Down to Click):

●   CTRL/right-click the words "Down State" in the Rollovers palette.

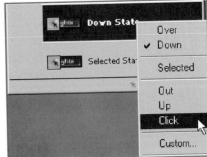

- CTRL/right-click the state (not the word) and select Set State from the pop up menu.

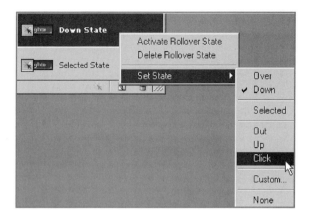

- Click the pop up menu in the top right corner of the Rollovers palette and select Rollover State Options. This will reveal the options dialog box.

- Double click the State to bring up the **Rollover State Options** dialog box.

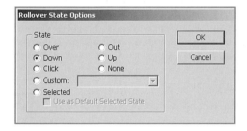

In each case you will be offered a selection of different states from which to choose. Some are self-explanatory, but others provide a very subtle difference in the way they function.

- **Over** – the image becomes active when the mouse cursor is over the image and the mouse button is not pressed.

- **Down** – the image becomes active when the mouse cursor is over the image and the mouse button is pressed down. The image remains active while the mouse button is depressed.

- **Click** – the image becomes active when the mouse cursor is over the image and the mouse button is clicked, which means the mouse button must be pressed down and released before the state is activated.

- **Custom** – if you know how to write JavaScript code and have embedded the code onto the html document, you can use this option to activate a named image when the user performs the action as designated in the JavaScript code.

- **Out** – literally, this would mean when the mouse curser is "out" or outside of the image and not touching it. It could describe the image before the user has actually even touched the mouse, so the normal initial slice would normally be used instead of using this state.

- **Up** – this refers to when the user has released the mouse button, and also describes the mouse button in its dormant mode. As with the previous option, the initial slice is normally used instead of this state.

- **None** – this maintains the state in its current image form, which can be used at a later time. This option will not create an image when the final optimised file is saved.

- **Selected** – the image becomes active after the mouse button is clicked. This state will remain until the user activates another selected rollover state. However other rollover states can still be operational while the selected state is active. For example, you would still want other rollover buttons to become active in the Up state on the web page.

If you want the Selected state to be active as soon as the page loads in the browser or when previewing in ImageReady, double-click the state and check the box labelled **Use as Default Selected State**.

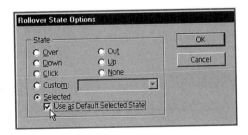

When you add a Selected State to a rollover, if you choose Click or Up for any of the other states you will see a warning triangle appear. This means the Selected State will override the Click and/or Up state.

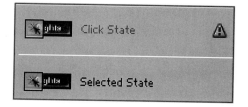

It is important to be aware that JavaScript is interpreted slightly differently by different makes and different versions of browsers. The events such as Down, Click, and Up may respond differently to clicks and double-clicks. The only way to assess what the user will see is to test the page in a variety of browsers, concentrating on the browser or browsers that you believe your target audience will be using.

Specifying URLs for image links

Once the rollover image has been completed, the URL to which it links can be assigned using the Slice palette in exactly the same way as in earlier versions of ImageReady. After selecting the relevant slice on the page, type the URL into the URL field in the Slice Palette.

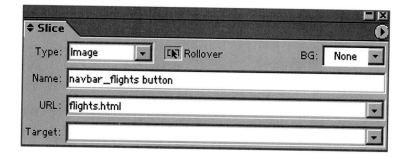

Rollover styles

The example navigation bar has two buttons, flights and hotels, but the actual navigation bar may have many more buttons. For the sake of good design practice and consistency it would be desirable to apply the same rollover effects to all of the buttons on the page. Rather than going through the same process for each button, you can create a style based on a complete rollover. This style can then be applied to any layer with just a click.

To demonstrate the process, use the rollover already created for the flights button. It is important that the rollover used as the basis for the style is a **layer-based** slice. The process used in the creation of the flights button automatically created a layer-based slice.

Creating and applying a rollover style

1. In the Rollovers palette, select any of the states that make up the rollover.

2. If the Styles palette is not visible go to Window > Styles. In the Styles palette click the **Create new style** icon at the bottom of the palette.

3. Type a name for the rollover. Make sure the **Include Rollover States** check box is checked. Check the other two check boxes if you want to include layer effects and blending options.

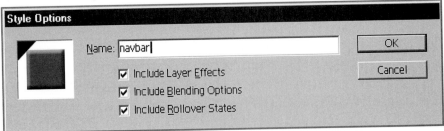

After clicking OK, the new style appears in the Styles palette. The initial state is shown in the thumbnail. The triangle in the top left corner of the thumbnail denotes the style is a rollover.

4. In the Layers palette, select the layer to which you want to apply the rollover style.

5. In the Styles palette, click the thumbnail of the style you want to apply.

The rollover will be applied to the artwork on the selected layer and the area sliced accordingly. The Rollovers palette will also be updated showing the latest rollover.

Copying, pasting, duplicating, and deleting states

Any state can be copied and pasted within the same rollover or between different rollovers. Unwanted states can also be deleted and states can be duplicated.

Select the state you are working with, and then click the pop up menu button in the top right corner of the palette.

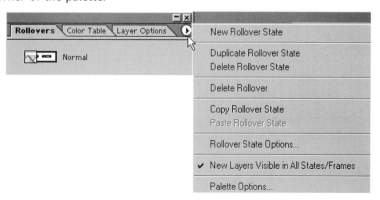

Select the required option from the pop up menu.

To paste a copied state, click the state you want to paste over and use the same pop up menu and select paste.

Creating animated rollovers

Animated rollovers provide a whole new level of dynamism to a page. They can be garish and gimmicky or sophisticated and informative, but you have the control and are only limited by your own imagination.

The concept of animated rollovers is based on the standard rollovers we have created in this chapter so far. The difference is that a self-contained animation based on a series of frames can be embedded within a state. When that state is activated in response to the users mouse action, they will see the animation play. This means an animation could be seen in the initial state of the button, but more commonly it would be used in the Over state. There is nothing to stop you using the Down state, but bear in mind the animation would need to be pretty rapid in order for it to be visible in the time it takes the user to click the mouse button.

Here is the artwork for the button that is going to be animated. Again, it can be downloaded from www.friendsofed.com and is called `anirollover.psd`. It is based on the same guidelines as the buttons in the previous sections. The artwork and text are on separate layers and a bevel effect has been applied to the artwork layer.

The rollover has been created with an Over and Down state. The Down state has a color change, but the Over state is the same as the initial normal slice. This is the state that is going to animate.

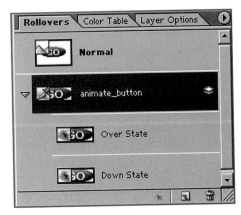

Animating a rollover

1. Select the state sub-layer in which you want to apply the animation. In this case it is the Over State.

2. Click the **Create animation frame** icon at the bottom of the Rollovers palette.

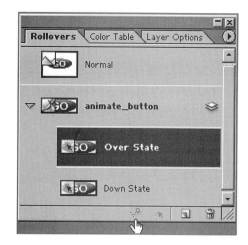

If this icon is not visible it will need to be enabled. Click the pop up menu button in the top right corner of the palette and select **Palette Options**. In the Options Palette check the **Include Animation Frames** check box.

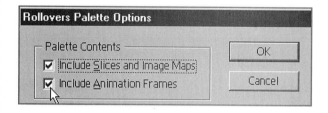

After clicking the Create Animation frame icon, two new states appear underneath the Over State. These are called Frame 1 and 2, and set up the basis for the animation. Any animation requires a minimum of two frames, one defining the start of the animation and one defining the end.

A two-frame animation can have a simple but effective influence on a web page, but it won't provide a wealth of possibilities. The more frames you have the more creative you can be, but at a cost. More frames means more images must be downloaded, adding to the page size. If the user moves the mouse away from the graphic quickly they may not see the full animation anyway.

Bearing that in mind, I am going to add a few more frames to this animation, just enough to make it more interesting, but not enough to weigh down the size of the page.

3. The Animation palette needs to play a role now. If it's not on your screen you can open it by going to Window > Animation.

    The Animation palette reflects the two frames in the Rollovers palette.

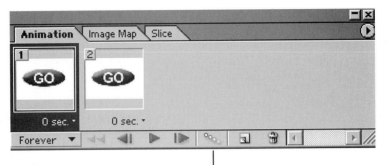

Tween frames

4. Select frame 1, either in the Animation palette or the Rollovers palette. Once a frame is selected the artwork relating to that frame can be edited. I used the Layer style icon in the Layers palette to change the button of frame 2 to a different color.

5. Click the **Tween animation frames** icon in the Animation palette.

6. In the Tween dialog box, select the options as in the image below. These elements are the same as in previous versions of ImageReady. These options tween frame 1 and 2, adding an additional 3 frames in between.

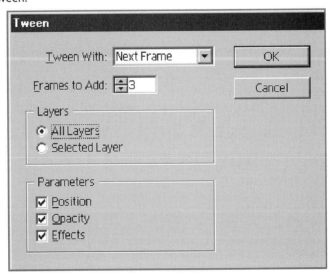

The result is a gradual blend of color between all five frames based on the original colors of frames 1 and 2.

You can now preview the rollover – you will see the color pulsating when the mouse is over the image.

Unifying and matching layers in rollovers

When editing states in rollovers, by default only the Selected state changes. There may be occasions when you want all the states in a rollover to conform to the artwork in one particular state, allowing you to edit anew from a different starting point.

In the Rollovers palette, select the state that you want all other states to conform to.

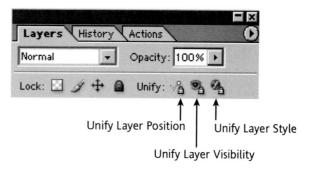

Unify Layer Position   Unify Layer Style

Unify Layer Visibility

In the Layers palette, three icons at the top of the page enable you to unify states by different means.

- Click the **Unify Layer Position** icon to reposition all other states to the same position as the selected state.

  A dialog box appears requesting your confirmation.

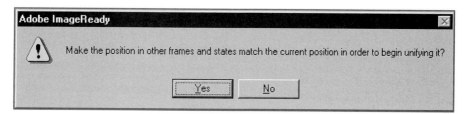

- Click the **Unify Layer Visibility** icon to show or hide all other states to match the selected state.

- Click the **Unify Layer Style** icon to copy styles from the selected state to all other states.

Conclusion

The new Rollovers palette is a significant addition to ImageReady 7.0 and simplifies what could be a highly complex task. As with any new technology, the boundary between function and design overkill can be a fine one, and careful attention to the target audience's needs and expectations should be a prime consideration.

Chapter 11

Managing Text

What we'll cover in this chapter:

- *Changes to the interface*

- *The introduction of multi-language support and dictionaries*

- *The Check Spelling feature*

- *Using the Find and Replace command*

- *New text anti-aliasing options*

- *Changes and additions to the Character palette*

The enhancements made to the text-handling capability of Photoshop may surprise users who see the application as primarily one for manipulating images. However, many designers now use Photoshop for preparing text-based web graphics. In version 7, the improvements in the text-handling capabilities, coupled with the enhancements allowing for selective optimization of text in web graphics (Chapter 9), can only increase the current trends towards using Photoshop as a total workflow solution.

*New features include the **multi-language** support, the related ability to **Check Spelling** in images, and the capability to perform **Find and Replace Text** options. This release also sees enhancements to text anti-aliasing, and additions to both the Character palette and menu.*

Interface changes

Although the Text tool options bar has not undergone a major change in content, a few cosmetic changes have been introduced.

- There is no longer an option for accessing the **Type Mask** tool from the options bar – this is now performed by choosing the tool from the standard toolbar. As with all the Photoshop tools, the various Type tools are grouped together in the Toolbox.

- Clicking on the **Type Orientation** button on the options bar changes type orientation. In previous versions, both vertical and horizontal icons were present. However, there is now only one button, which is enabled when you have added text to your design, and clicking on it will automatically change the orientation.

- You can access the Character and Paragraph palettes by either clicking on the new **Palette** icon on the right of the Type tool options bar, or by choosing the palettes from the Window menu as before.

Multi-language support

The support for multiple languages within Photoshop is integral to the usefulness of the new Spell Check feature. Photoshop 7 is shipped with a number of foreign language dictionaries, and with the increasing demand for design that can be repurposed for international use, Photoshop's support for these languages in a Spell Check feature becomes even more important.

As well as choosing to set your language specific to the document, you can also set separate layers to different languages, or even have a mixture on the same layer. This becomes important when entire websites need to be built in different language versions, where separate parts of an image or website are set in different languages, or even where foreign words have standard usage in different languages. Access to the various languages that have been included is achieved through the drop down menu at the base of the Character palette.

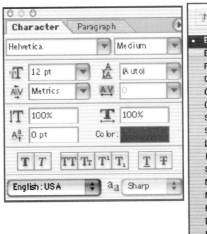

Text can be assigned a language in a number of ways:

- Using the type tool, highlight type that has already been created, and select a language from the drop-down menu at the base of the Character palette. This can be performed on individual words, sentences, or paragraphs.

- Highlight the Type layer in the Layers palette and then choose a language from the drop-down menu to assign a language to a layer.

- Select the language you wish to use and then create the type, switching languages as needed within a sentence or paragraph.

Using the Spell Checker

In line with other Adobe applications, Photoshop now includes support for checking spelling in a number of different languages. As mentioned previously, the development of the web specific features of Photoshop and the consequent increase in the use of type in both jpeg and gif images necessitated the inclusion of such a feature.

If you are familiar with Spell Checks in other applications, you will notice that the Photoshop Spell Check offers features common to those in most other programs. When you run the Spell Check, Photoshop will check the words and list alternatives for those words it does not recognize. You then have the following options: Ignore, Ignore All, Change, Change All, to amend the spelling by typing into the Change To field, and to Add the word to the list. We will look at these options in further detail later in the chapter.

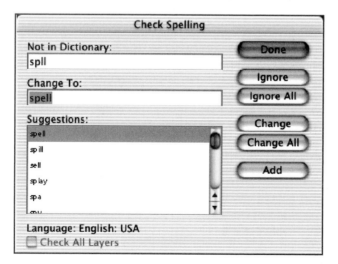

Selecting the type to be checked

The Spell Check command is located on the Edit menu, but before you attempt to check the spelling in an image, you need to decide the type that Photoshop will evaluate.

- If you wish to check all the type in an image, select Edit > Check Spelling. Prior to running the spell checker, you need to determine if the type is on multiple layers. If so, you should double-check that all type layers are visible. Spell Check in Photoshop will ignore type that is on hidden layers therefore corrections will not be made. You will be alerted to this the first time you attempt to check the spelling on a hidden type layer, but the dialog box does have one of those handy 'Don't show again' options, and if you check this, you'll need to remember this limitation for future use.

  Also, if the file does have multiple type layers, then you should check the **Check All Layers** option.

- If you wish to check all the spelling on a particular layer, make that layer active in the Layers palette and then choose the Spell Check command. If your file has multiple type layers, ensure that the Check All Layers option is not checked.

- To limit your spell check to specific text on a layer, highlight the text before you run the Spell Check command.

Responding to the Spell Check dialog box

With the target type chosen, select Edit > Check Spelling. The Check Spelling dialog box will open, and Photoshop will list the first word that it assumes to be misspelled in the **Not in Dictionary** field.

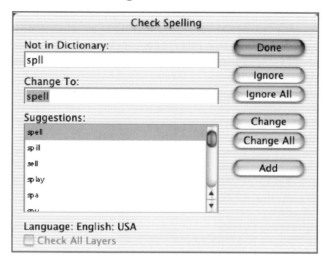

In the screenshot shown, Photoshop has located the word 'spll' in the type, assumed that this word is incorrect, and displayed an alternate word in the **Change To** field. You then have the following options:

- If the word is correctly spelt and you feel no need to add the word to the dictionary, choose the **Ignore** option to ignore just that occurrence.

- If you want Photoshop to ignore any further occurrences of that word in the type, select **Ignore All**.

- Assuming that the word is a spelling mistake, and you want Photoshop to make the changes, there are a number of steps to be followed:

  - If the correct word is displayed in the **Change To** field, select **Change** to change just that occurrence, or **Change All** to change any further occurrences.

  - If the alternate word displayed was not correct, you could choose the correct option by scrolling down the list of **Suggestions** and clicking on the desired option before choosing Change or Change All. Alternatively, you can type the correct spelling in the Change To field and then choose Change or Change All.

- Finally, if the word was correctly spelt and you know that you will be using that particular terminology often, you could choose **Add** to add the word to the dictionary, and stop Photoshop from seeing the word as a spelling error. It would then pick up if you misspelled it later.

Photoshop will continue to check the type, moving on to each suspect word in turn until it has completed the Spell Check. On completion of the process, a dialog box is displayed which informs you that the Spell Check is complete. Once again, it has an option that the dialog box is not displayed again, but I'd suggest that you did not check this so that each time you run a spell check, you can be confident that the process has been completed.

If at any stage you wish to terminate the Spell Check process, either select **Done** or close the Check Spelling dialog box.

Type that has been rasterized, converted to a shape, or created with the Type Mask tool cannot be checked.

Checking the Piccolo site

Located in the Sample folder within the Photoshop application is a multi-layer image complete with sufficient type for you to see how the Spell Check feature works.

1. Open `Piccolo Site.psd`. Notice how in the Layers palette there are a number of Layer sets and that within these Layer sets there are Type layers that have been hidden.

2. Without making any of the Type layers visible, select Edit > Check Spelling. Notice the warning dialog box that appears regarding invisible Type layers. Choose Skip for this and all further boxes, until you enter the Spell Check dialog. (Note here why you might want to permanently disable them!)

3. Expand the Recipes Layer set, and make the Pasta Rollover Text visible. Choose Edit > Check Spelling and then deselect Check All Layers to restrict the spell check to the current layer. The word linguini will be shown as Not in Dictionary, but as you know it to be correct and wish to add it to the dictionary, choose Add.

4. The next 'error' to be highlighted is the word F, as in Fahrenheit. Although you know this abbreviation to be correct, you don't wish to add it to the dictionary, so choose Ignore or Ignore All.

5. Those are the only two 'errors' on that layer, and Photoshop will display the command that the Spell Check is complete. Unless of

course, you have already run the Spell Check before, and have chosen that this dialog box is not selected.

6.   Expand the Guest Chefs Layer set, and highlight the Guest Chefs Rollover Text layer. Run the Check Spelling command, and you'll notice that the only words highlighted are the names of the chef and the article author. Look closely at the last paragraph and you'll notice some Italian text, yet these words were not highlighted as errors.

7.   With the Type tool, click in either or both of the words 'Molto Bene', and if you look at the base of the Character palette, you'll notice that these words have been tagged as being Italian, and so they were checked against the Italian dictionary when the Spell Check was run.

Using the Find and Replace Text command

Expanding on the improved text handling capabilities of this version is the introduction of the **Find and Replace Text** command. Once again it may seem a little out of place to have such a powerful text tool in an image-editing application, but if we return to that imaginary situation of having to create a website which can be re-purposed for different regions, the strength of this tool becomes apparent.

In the case of the Piccolo website you just investigated, imagine Piccolo markets are a US-based concern. Not wishing to limit their appeal, they have decided to re-work the site to be suitable for all English speaking markets. This means the measurements and temperatures need to be converted from Imperial to metric. This could be done either manually, which is time-consuming and all too often inaccurate, or by using the Find and Replace command.

Determining the type to be searched

As with the Check Spelling command, you'll need to evaluate which type should be searched and the parameters for the search before you run the Find and Replace command.

Once again, Photoshop will only search the type on Type layers that are visible. Thus you should ensure that all layers to be checked have been made visible before you run the command, or run the command multiple times. There is a warning dialog box if some layers are not visible, but you can switch this warning off.

Establishing the search criteria

Having decided which layers will be visible, ensure that one of those visible layers is active and then choose Edit > Find and Replace Text.

Once the Find and Replace Text dialog box appears, you have a number of options to select before you actually run the command on the text in your document:

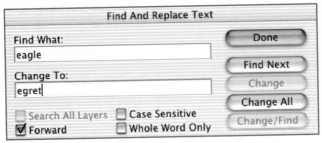

- In the **Find What** field, type the letter, letters, word, or group of words you wish to find.

- In the **Change To** field, type the new replacement text.

- To check all visible type layers in a file, check the **Search All Layers** option at the base of the dialog box. Note that if the file has a single type layer, the option will be grayed out as indicated in the screenshot above.

- Checking the **Forward** option means that Photoshop will only search the text from the insertion point onwards, it does not loop back through the text to the beginning of the paragraph. However if there is no insertion point in the text, this will not make any difference.

- If you wish the search to be case-sensitive, check the **Case Sensitive** option. This means that the text will only find and then replace words that correspond exactly with regard to upper and lower case letters.

- Selecting the **Whole Word Only** option restricts the search to returning only complete words that correspond to your search criteria. If you entered 'art' in the Find What field, and left Whole Word unchecked, Photoshop would find words such as heart, artistic, and artist, but by checking Whole Word Only the word art would be found.

Performing Find and Replace

Once all the options have been selected as needed, you are then in a position to effectively search through the text and have Photoshop find and replace the target words.

- To begin the search, depress the **Find Next** button. Photoshop will search and then highlight the first occurrence of the Find What text. If you cannot see the highlighted text, it may be that the dialog box is covering the text and needs to be moved.

- If you select **Change**, the target text will be replaced with the text in the Change To field, and the search will not continue until you click the Find Next button again.

- Using the **Change/Find** option is often preferable to selecting Change because it eliminates the need to repeatedly continue the search by pressing Find Next. Each time you choose Change/Find, the text will be replaced and the next occurrence highlighted.

- **Change All** will search through the entire image, taking into account limitations set by visible layers and the Check All Layers option, and will automatically replace all occurrences of the found text.

- Choosing **Done** will close the dialog box. You can opt to do this at any stage in the process, or when Photoshop has displayed a dialog box informing you that all text has been searched and how many replacements have been made.

Once again if you do not have a text-heavy image at hand, it may be useful for you to open the `Piccolo Site.psd` file in the Samples folder and run a Find and Replace command, bearing in mind all the points which have been mentioned.

New text anti-aliasing options

Although text anti-aliasing options are not new to this version of Photoshop, a further option has been introduced.

The newest addition to this menu is the **Sharp** option, which creates text that is sharper than the previous Crisp option.

Remember that in using anti-aliasing on text for web graphics you will increase the size of the file. Also when setting online text at small sizes, you should deselect the Fractional Width option in the Character palette menu if the text seems to be rendered inconsistently.

Enhancements to the Character palette and menu

Although little has changed in this palette, some useful features have been added. The new support for multiple language dictionaries has already been discussed, but there are a number of other changes that should be immediately noticeable.

The options for enhancing type by using Faux Bold, Faux Italic, and other formatting styles still exist on the Character palette menu. They are now also visible near the base of the Character palette, eliminating the need to access the menu if you wish to apply any of these styles. The options are from left to right:

- Faux Bold
- Faux Italic
- All Caps
- Small Caps
- Superscript
- Subscript
- Underline
- Strikethrough

Also added to the base of the Character palette is an option to choose the level of anti-aliasing applied to text, which means it can now be accessed from the Type tool options bar, the Layer > Type submenu, or the Character palette.

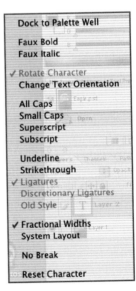

Added to the Character palette menu is the option to **Change Text Orientation**, so it can now be accessed either from this menu or the Type tool options bar.

Two new features for handling type are support for **Discretionary Ligatures** and the **System Layout** command.

Using discretionary ligatures

Previous editions of Photoshop supported the use of standard ligatures in type, a common example being the fi and fl ligatures where special characters were used to avoid any unsightly collisions between these letters. However some OpenType® fonts are now providing ligatures additional to those in common use. Known as discretionary ligatures, these could include ligatures for **ct**, **sp**, and **st** character combinations.

Adobe and Microsoft teamed up to produce OpenType® fonts in the late 1990s to try to overcome the limitations of the two major type formats available at that time. Basically, both type formats suffered from typographic and platform problems. OpenType® solves both of these, it is a cross-platform type (can be used on both Mac and Windows), and it can contain more than 65,000 characters, which allow for additional flourishes to the font being used.

If your font supports them, you can display them in your type by checking Discretionary Ligatures on the Character palette menu.

More information about OpenType® fonts, their features, availability, and system requirements can be found in the OpenType User Guide (`OTGuide.pdf`) recently located at www.adobe.com/type/browsers/pdfs/OTGuide.pdf.

Using system layout

If you are using Photoshop to design elements for user interfaces, for example menus, warning and dialog boxes, switching this command on will display the text using your operating systems default text handling. This means that you'll get a more accurate representation of how these interface elements will be viewed by a user.

Notice that when using System Layout, all anti-aliasing will be removed from the text.

Conclusion

Although Photoshop is not primarily a type-handling tool, these improvements to the functionality in version 7 are a welcome addition. They will help designers to reliably create those text heavy images both for print and web, completely within Photoshop, rather than having to enlist the help of a word processing package.

Chapter 12

Creating Web Galleries and Picture Packages

What we'll cover in this chapter:

- *Creating Web photo galleries*

- *Defining style options*

- *Defining settings for text information and security*

- *Creating Picture Packages*

- *Creating multiple image Picture Packages*

All designers and illustrators have to be able to display their work, and the Photoshop features **Web Galleries** and **Picture Packages** are ideal ways to do this, for people who want quick and easy solutions, without the need to learn other programs.

Although neither feature is totally new to Photoshop, there have been real improvements in this version in terms of the functionality of both, particularly in regards to security of images in web galleries, and economy when printing images, using picture packages.

Creating web galleries

While this is not a new feature to Photoshop 7, it has been extended to offer a broader range of options, including more templates for viewing galleries, and greater options for providing information about the image, creator, or even general information. Most notably, this new information can include important security measures such as copyrights and watermarks, which can be automatically generated, helping you to prevent unlawful use of your images.

Photoshop's web galleries provide the fastest way to create an online portfolio of all your work without having to do any html coding or file preparation. All your images, formats, and sizes will be automatically converted and resized ready to be incorporated into a neat, simple, and user-friendly interface.

Your only task is to put all your required images into a source folder and create a destination folder into which the new optimized files will be saved.

Once you have your folders ready, go to File > Automate > Web Photo Gallery.

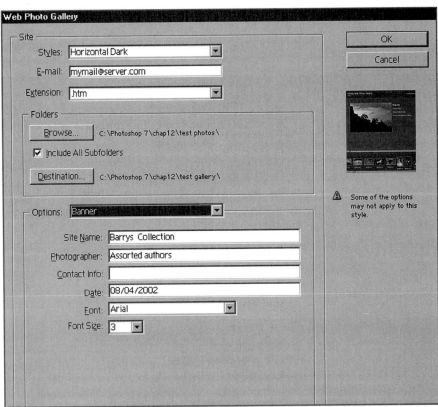

The dialog box is where you specify the kind of gallery you want to create as well as the information that you want to appear by entering the information into the following fields:

■ **Styles** – this drop down box describes the template that will be generated as html code, enabling the gallery to be viewed in any web browser.

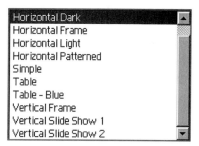

As you select different templates, the preview window to the right of the drop down box updates, showing you what the page will look like.

All templates are based on an index of clickable thumbnail images that link through to full size images. What "full size" means can be determined by you, as you will see shortly. Some templates even generate an automated slide show, with each image updating every 10 seconds.

■ **E-mail** – if desired, enter an email address that will appear on the web page as a hypertext link.

■ **Extension** – you can choose either .htm or .html as the suffix to the web page file names. If the gallery is going to be incorporated in a larger web site, it is good practice to ensure the file extension is consistent with the other pages in the site. Generally, .html is considered more cross-platform compatible.

■ **Browse** button – click to navigate to the source folder holding your images. Check the **Include All Subfolders** check box if you wish to add sub folders to the gallery.

- **Destination** button – click to navigate to the destination folder where your newly saved images will be stored. This must be a different folder to your source folder, or you will see this warning dialog:

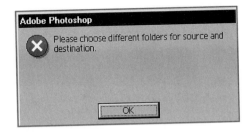

- **Options** – this is where you have a degree of customization in terms of text, image sizes, colors, and fonts. The options are summarized below:

  - **Banner** – this allows you to add a banner to your page.

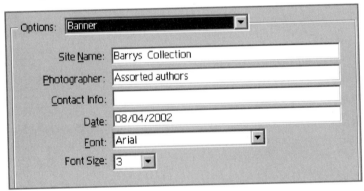

The **Site Name** will be the text that appears as the heading on the page.

If required, you can use the **Photographer** and **Contact Info** fields to enter this information. These will not appear on the page.

The **Date** is the current date by default, but can be overtyped.

Finally, you can select the **Font** and **Font Size**. Font sizes are html sizes, not point sizes. Size 3 is the default size for web pages, but you can select any size from size 1 (smallest) to size 7 (largest).

- **Large Images** – if you want all images to be resized to a common format, check the **Resize Images** check box so additional drop down boxes and numeric fields become enabled.

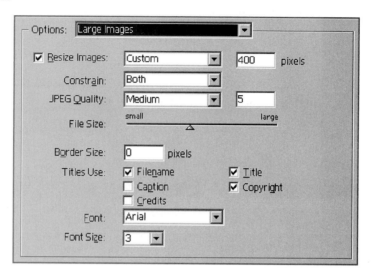

Here Custom has been selected. This allows you to enter a pixel value. The other options are Small (250 px), Medium (350 px), or Large (450 px). Although there is no way, at this time, to save custom settings, what you enter here will remain if you go back to use this feature again. This is handy if you prefer not to use the default settings.

The **Constrain** drop down box allows to you specify whether the pixel value you have typed refers to the width or the height. If you select Both, the pixel value will be applied to whichever is the greater.

JPEG Quality uses the jpeg algorithm to convert the images. Either select from Low to Maximum, or type a number, or use the slider labeled **File Size**. Higher values result in higher quality, but greater file size. Quality 5 offers a good compromise, but testing is the only way to be sure.

Border Size adds a pixel-based border around each image.

The check boxes listed in the **Titles Use** section refer to information saved with the original images. If you want to use this feature, prepare your images by going to File > File Info and filling in the dialog box as required, before saving. Once information has been saved with each image, the information can be displayed in the gallery by checking the relevant check box.

Finally, you can select the font and size you wish the text to be rendered at. Again, sizes are html sizes, not point measurements.

- **Thumbnails** – this defines the settings for thumbnail images.

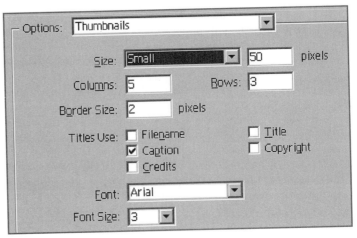

Select the desired **Size** or choose Custom to specify your own size.

Columns and **Rows** are used to define the configuration for the html table that will be used to layout the thumbnail images on the home page. These will not apply when Horizontal or Vertical Frame Styles are used.

Apply a **Border Size** for the thumbnail if desired.

The other settings are identical to the previous section.

- **Custom Colors** – this allows you to choose the color scheme of your page.

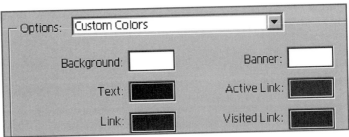

If colors are not specified in the chosen style, new page **Background** and **Banner** colors can be set from here. Additionally **Text** and **Link** colors can be changed from the default colors by clicking each color swatch. The only options that are not totally self explanatory are **Active Link**, which refers to the color of the link while the user's mouse button is depressed, and **Visited Link**, which refers to the color of the link after it has been selected, showing the user that they have already visited the corresponding page.

■ **Security** – this enables you to specify text to appear across the image in a number of formats.

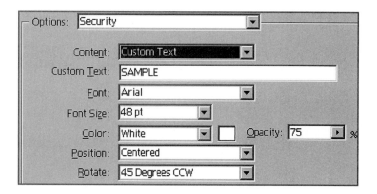

The **Content** drop down box allows you to specify such things as Caption, Copyright, title, etc. Once again this information is taken from the file information saved with each image. If you do not want any text to appear across the image select None here.

In the picture above, **Custom Text** has been selected. In the Custom Text field I have entered the word SAMPLE.

Select the desired **Font**, **Size**, **Color**, **Opacity**, **Position**, and what angle you want it to be **Rotated**, as it appears on top of the image. I wanted the text to be partially transparent and diagonal across the image.

The picture below shows how an image appears in the gallery, based on the settings I used.

The following image shows the finished gallery in a web browser complete with thumbnails, and copyright information. This gallery was created using the Horizontal Dark Style and the color image can be seen in the color section of the book.

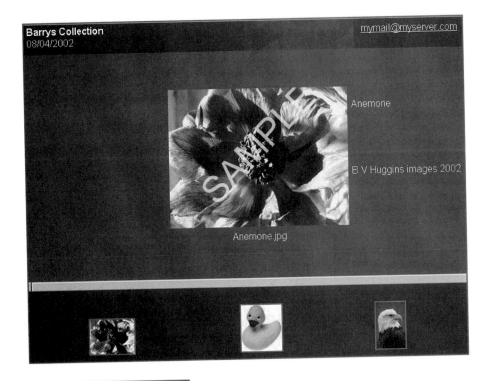

This gallery is now a permanent set of files and can be opened independently of Photoshop within a web browser. The picture shows the file structure that was created on my PC. The folder I created was named test gallery. All the files and folders within that folder were named and created by Photoshop. The file called `index.htm` is the main home page. Double-clicking this file will open the gallery in the web browser.

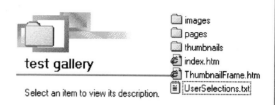

The included gallery styles offer a broad range of options suiting most needs, but styles can be edited further to customize your gallery as much as you need. All the files created are html documents, so each page can be edited using an ordinary text editor if you write html, or by opening the pages in a web page creation application such as Dreamweaver or GoLive.

Creating Picture Packages

As well as being a great time saver, the Picture Package command helps you cut costs by printing multiple images on one sheet of paper in a variety of configurations. In version 7, it is even possible to place different images on the same page.

Additionally, further information such as copyrights and captions can be printed as labels with each image in a similar way to web galleries.

A range of layouts are available to use as preset templates, but you can also create your own layouts using any text editing application. To create a Picture Package layout go to File > Automate > Picture Package.

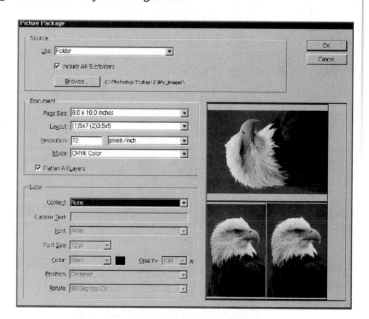

- To create a batch of picture packages, select **Folder** from the **Use** drop down box. The other options are **File**, to use a specified file only, and **Frontmost Document**, to use the current active image.

- Click the **Browse** button to navigate to the required folder.

- The **Document** section allows you to define the printed page size, the Layout configuration, resolution, and color mode.

- Checking the **Flatten All Layers** check box creates a file with all layers flattened onto one layer.

- The **Label** section allows information to be added to the images in a similar way to web galleries.

- The **Content** drop down box offers labels including copyright, title, caption, and a custom text option.

- The preview on the right of the dialog box shows the configuration for the chosen page layout. However, as with web galleries, only the image content will appear.

Click OK and a page will be created for each file from within the source folder, in the specified layout.

Creating a picture package with different images

Following the same steps as for creating a standard picture package, place the cursor over any thumbnail in the preview window and click. From the dialog box that opens, which will be the standard Open dialog of your operating system, select the file you wish to include. Files may be selected from any location and do not have to be in the same folder.

Conclusion

Apart from the added functionality of the enhanced web gallery features, one of the most welcome additions comes in the form of the new security options. While illegal copying and fraudulent use of images on the web will always be difficult to combat, any measures that make the practice difficult to carry out, whilst still allowing you to market your work, are a step in the right direction.

Cost cutting has also been addressed by Adobe in version 7, with the revamped Picture Package command. The new ability to print multiple images at different sizes will offer significant long-term savings, whether using commercial printing, or filling up a page of expensive coated paper for use in a personal printer.

Chapter 13

Scripting in Photoshop

What we'll cover in this chapter:

- *Scripting documentation*

- *Scripts vs Actions*

- *Installing Scripting Support on both the Mac and Windows platforms*

- *Running JavaScripts from within Photoshop*

- *Accessing JavaScripts from within Photoshop*

- *Writing and debugging JavaScripts for Photoshop*

- *Using Visual Basic and AppleScript scripts*

- *Using the Scripting Listener*

The introduction of scripting support for Photoshop, and the ability to run JavaScript scripts from within Photoshop, or external Visual Basic and AppleScript scripts on Photoshop images, may seem a digression from the primary role of the application – that of image editing. However, as production needs develop, especially with regard to preparing images for the web or designing in complex workflows, the need to automate repetitive processes effectively becomes more and more apparent.

Although an in-depth coverage of how to write scripts is far beyond the scope of this book, what we will do in this chapter is explain where and how scripts and scripting support is installed, the usefulness of scripts in automating the production process, a short comparison between the functionality of Actions and Scripts, and how to run scripts from within Photoshop, coupled with information on where you can find out more.

The introduction of Actions in recent years, and the facility to use those actions to Batch Process images within folders was the first step towards automation. The Scripting function just takes that one step further, unleashing the power of various scripting languages – AppleScript, Visual Basic and JavaScript – allowing for the creation of efficient, complex, and, in the instance of JavaScript, cross-platform scripts.

If you are a designer with little or no experience of scripting, you may well be thinking that the prospect of learning to script is too daunting and that you'll have little need for it. However, if you think about how useful actions have become for automating your repetitive production workflows, the strength of scripting will soon become apparent. A word of advice when you start to try and script is to start slowly, write simple, short scripts and build your knowledge from there. Another pointer is to look at scripts that have already been created, run them on your images, as we will do a little later in this chapter, and then look at both the History palette and the actual script in text format and try and discover what is happening. It is easier to amend existing scripts to suit your purposes than it is to write them from scratch.

If you are an experienced scripter – be it JavaScript, AppleScript or Visual Basic – learning how to script for Photoshop will be a relatively painless procedure. The most important new aspect for you to assimilate will be **objects** as they exist within Photoshop, and then you'll be well on your way to creating scripts for the application.

Scripts vs actions

If, as was suggested a little earlier, there is a similarity between automating the production process using actions, and automating using scripts, you may well be asking why scripting support has been introduced, and whether it will be of any use to you.

When you 'run' an action, the commands that have been recorded for that action are played in a linear process. Photoshop completes each command in turn, running through the action from start to finish.

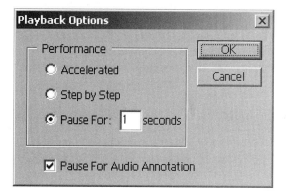

To see this in action, change the Playback options to those illustrated in the screenshot above. Expand the action within the palette and then run the action, noting how each part of the action is played in the order in which it was created.

Using scripts, we are not confined to this linear process because we have access to **conditional** statements. In other words, we tell Photoshop to check for a certain setting and only execute the script if that setting is as we want it. In plain English – if this is true, do that, but if it is not true, do something else. We'll be having a look at the concept of conditional statements a little later on in this chapter.

The second strength of scripting is that we can use scripts to develop more complex workflows by telling the script to not only target an image within Photoshop, but also to save and open that image in another application that supports scripting, such as Adobe Illustrator. With actions we do not have this power – we are limited to running the action on the active image only, or using the action in Batch Processing and targeting specific folders and sub-folders.

Installing Adobe Photoshop Scripting Support

Before you attempt to use any scripts with Photoshop, you will need to make sure the Scripting Support plug-in is installed, as it is not yet an integral part of Photoshop. The Scripting function is located on the File > Automate submenu, and if you check this menu you'll know whether or not Scripting Support has been installed on the machine. If the option is not visible, and you wish to take advantage of this new Scripting Support function, you'll need to install it yourself.

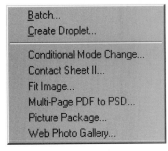

Scripting Support not installed   Scripting Support installed

The Scripting support plug-in is not included on the CD for version 7.0. At the time of going to press, it is available as a download from the Adobe website at the following addresses:

http://download.adobe.com/pub/adobe/photoshop/mac/7.x/photoshop_scripting_10.img.hqx (Mac)

http://download.adobe.com/pub/adobe/photoshop/win/7.x/photoshop_scripting_10.exe (PC)

If you have installed PhotoScripter on your machine, you will need to remove the PhotoScripter plug-in from the Photoshop Plug-Ins folder, as it is not compatible with Scripting Support.

If during the installation process, you had Adobe Photoshop open, it is recommended that you close and restart the application. On reloading Photoshop, a glance at the File > Automate submenu should show that Scripting Support has been installed by adding the option to the bottom of the submenu.

Scripting documentation

In order for you to get the best from this new Scripting Support, extensive documentation explaining both scripting within Photoshop and specific scripting language requirements have also been installed in the Photoshop Scripting 1 folder along with the plug-in. These files are in pdf format, for which you'll need to have Acrobat or Acrobat Reader installed, and they are located within the Documentation folder, and additionally within other folders.

Sample scripts and other utilities are also contained within additional folders.

Another thing to note is that when you have installed Scripting Support on Windows, if you created droplets with Photoshop 6 or earlier versions, they will no longer work. You can use droplets created in Photoshop 7.0 with the Scripting Support installed, and if you uninstall it your earlier droplets will work again. To uninstall on a Mac, take the Scripting folder out of the plug-ins folder, the Scripts folder out of the Presets folder, and the Adobe Unit Types scripting addition from the Scripting Additions folder. From Windows, you can use the Control Panel and Add/Remove programs.

JavaScript scripts within Photoshop

Obviously, once you have installed Scripting Support, you'll need to know how to access and run various JavaScripts, and where to store any additional JavaScripts within Photoshop so that you can access them easily from within the Scripts dialog box.

Once you have completed the installation of the Scripting Support plug-in, a limited number of pre-created scripts will also have been installed. We'll use the default scripts as a starting point, and then we'll show you how and where to save additional scripts.

Before you run any of the installed scripts, you'll need to have an image open. You can obviously select a file of your own, or use one of the images that have been supplied in the Samples folder. As we'll be having a look at the History palette a little later on, I'd suggest that you open a new file, so that the only actions represented in the History palette are those that have occurred as a result of running the script.

As you begin to learn more about scripting, and even run some pre-created scripts on your images, it is handy to have the History palette open so that you have a step-by-step account of what the script has done to your image. This is a useful tool for learning more about scripts, although in some instances, not all of the script's actions will be reflected in the History palette.

Running JavaScripts from within Photoshop

1. With an image open, choose   File   > Automate > Scripts to display the Scripts dialog box.

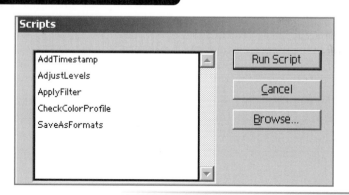

2. Select the ApplyFilter script and click on the **Run Script** button. The script will run, and all the instructions contained within the script will be executed. What you should notice is that a Motion Blur filter has been applied to different sections of the image. An inspection of the History palette will show you exactly what happened when you ran this script.

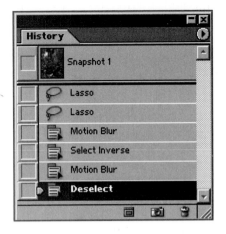

You will notice that two selections were created using the Lasso tool and a Motion Blur filter was applied to these selections. The selection was then inversed, and a Motion Blur was applied to the remaining sections. Finally the selections were deselected. What you cannot see in the History palette are the dimensions for the selections or the values which were applied to the Motion Blur filter, but breaking a script apart like this will give you that first hint at understanding what was in the script. You can go backwards through the History palette, removing one history state at a time, to see what has happened to your image in a bit more detail.

If you're a little more experienced with creating your own scripts, or curious about how they work, you may wish to have a look at the script and the commands used to create the previous manipulation.

Note that anything enclosed within /*...*/ or lines of code starting with // are comments – although they appear in the script itself they are for reference and are ignored by the application when it runs the script. You can look at them to get a clearer idea of which part of the code performs each part of the function.

Here is the code:

```
if ( documents.length > 0 )
{
            /*
This function applies a motion blur filter to each of the
4 quadrants in the front most image. The resulting effect
is a combined motion blur with a center in the center of
the image
*/
```

```
var docRef = activeDocument;
if(              docRef.bitsPerChannel ==
BitsPerChannelType.EIGHT &&
(               docRef.mode == DocumentMode.CMYK        ||
docRef.mode == DocumentMode.RGB ||
docRef.mode == DocumentMode.LAB ) )
{
var mySelectionWidth = docRef.width / 2;
var mySelectionHeight = docRef.height / 2;

//Select the top-left and bottom right corner
docRef.selection.select(new Array(    new Array(0, 0),
new Array(0, mySelectionHeight),
new Array(mySelectionWidth, mySelectionHeight ),
new Array(mySelectionWidth, 0)),
SelectionType.REPLACE, 0, false)

docRef.selection.select(new Array(    new
Array(mySelectionWidth, mySelectionHeight),
new Array(mySelectionWidth, docRef.height),
new Array(docRef.width, docRef.height ),
new Array(docRef.width, mySelectionHeight)),
SelectionType.EXTEND, 0, false)

// Apply the motion blur filter
docRef.activeLayer.applyMotionBlur( -45, 45 );

// Select the opposite corners
docRef.selection.invert();

// Apply the motion blur filter with an orthogonal direc-
tion
docRef.activeLayer.applyMotionBlur( 45, 45 );

docRef.selection.deselect();
}
else
{
alert( "This function only operates on 8 bit RGB, CMYK or
Lab documents" );
}
}
else
{
alert( "You must have a document open to add a time-
stamp!" );
}
```

Having a look at that coding might seem pretty complex if this is the first time you've ever seen JavaScript code, so we'll keep our dissection of it at a simple level. What you may notice is that right at the beginning of the code, there is a sentence that says:

```
if ( documents.length > 0 )
```

This is what we would term a conditional statement, in that the script will only execute the command within the braces {} – everything apart from the last four lines – if the argument between the parenthesis is true, and the number of documents open is greater than 0.

What happens is that the script will run, evaluate the number of open documents, and, if there is at least one document open, it will execute the code. However, if no document is open, then the argument is not true, and it will miss out all the code inside that particular set of braces and jump to the end, where the partner to the `if` command, the `else` command, is located.

Note that this is the basic structure of all programming languages – they are nested so that a command at the beginning will have its partner at the end, the second command will have its partner code second from bottom, and so on.

The script will then execute the following code:

```
else
{
alert( "You must have a document open to add a
timestamp!" );
}
```

3. Close all your open images, and run the `ApplyFilter` script again by choosing File > Automate > Scripts, and **ApplyFilter** from within the Script dialog box. As you have no document open, all the code within that set of braces as indicated above will not be executed, and you see an alert dialog box as follows:

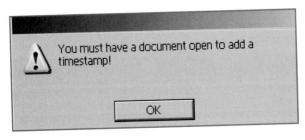

As you have probably noticed, the text that's displayed in this alert box is actually incorrect, because we are running the ApplyFilter script, and yet the warning refers to timestamps. You can correct it yourself at this stage if you wish, or even add your own custom alert message.

Editing the ApplyFilter script

To edit the ApplyFilter script, you'll need to locate the file on your hard drive and then open it within any Text Editor, Simple Text will work fine on the Mac, and Notepad is suitable on a Windows machine.

1. Launch your text editor.

2. From the File menu, choose Open and then navigate through your hard drive to the Photoshop 7\Presets\Scripts folder. If you cannot see the `ApplyFilter.js` file, you may need to instruct the application to show all files.

3. Open the `ApplyFilter.js` file, and scroll to the bottom of the document until you see the last alert text.

4. Change the text from "`You must have a document open to add a timestamp!`" to "`You must have a document open to run this filter command`". Note you must ensure that you retain the quotation marks, and that the new text to be displayed appears within those quotation marks.

5. Save the file as `ApplyFilter2.js` in the Photoshop 7\Presets\Scripts folder and close the text editor.

6. From within Photoshop, once again ensuring that you have no files open, run the `ApplyFilter2` script using File > Automate > Scripts and choosing the script from the list displayed in the dialog box. Note that because you saved the file into the Scripts folder, it is automatically displayed.

7. On running the script, the alert that is displayed should now contain the corrected text.

Granted, that was a very simple correction to an existing JavaScript file, but if you're new to the concept, hopefully it sparked an interest and slightly lessened any apprehension you were feeling about learning to script. If you are experienced, you've now had a chance to look at a JavaScript file that will run within Photoshop, and seen some of the Photoshop objects. You can find a full listing of JavaScript Photoshop objects in the JavaScript reference pdf.

One last look at that code. Notice the alert that preceded the comment about having a document open:

```
else
{
alert( "This function only operates on 8 bit RGB, CMYK or
Lab documents" );
}
```

Drawing on what you have already learned about how scripts function, you may already have deduced that this command is going to display an alert if the image is not an 8bit RGB, CMYK or Lab document. But you may be asking where in the preceding code the instruction to check the mode and bit depth was issued.

```
if(            docRef.bitsPerChannel ==
BitsPerChannelType.EIGHT &&
(            docRef.mode == DocumentMode.CMYK       ||
docRef.mode == DocumentMode.RGB ||
docRef.mode == DocumentMode.LAB ) )
```

There it is, another conditional statement! Photoshop is being instructed to check that the document is an 8 bit document and also that the document is either in CMYK, RGB or Lab mode. Only if both parts of the argument – the bit depth and the color mode are true, will the code within the braces execute. Failing that, it will jump to the alert preceded by the first else statement.

```
else
{
alert( "This function only operates on 8 bit RGB, CMYK or
Lab documents" );
}
```

Test this by opening a grayscale image, such as `Old Image.jpg` from the Photoshop samples folder, and running the ApplyFilter script. You should be confronted with the alert text that we have been discussing above.

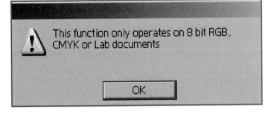

It is this concept of conditional statements mentioned earlier that makes the concept of scripting so much more powerful and useful than Actions. If you look at the sample script we have been studying, two conditional statements were included in the script. The first was the check that was run to see if one or more than one document was open, and the second was checking for the bit depth and color mode of the image that was open. If we show this as a flowchart, you'll see that the process is as follows.

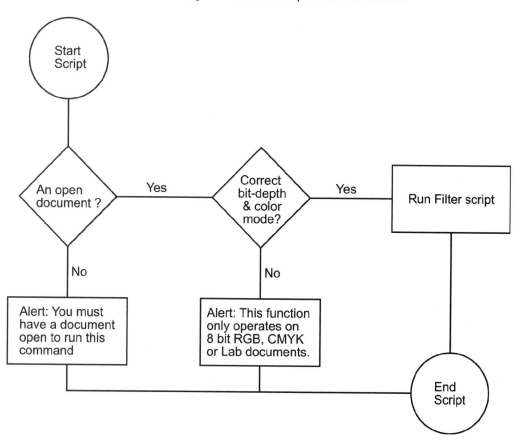

Unlike working with Actions, which run sequentially through a set of recorded commands, using scripts we can assess whether conditions have been met, and have the script make decisions based on those conditions.

Accessing JavaScripts from within Photoshop

In the earlier exercise, we accessed the ApplyFilter script by choosing File > Automate > Scripts and choosing the ApplyFilter script from the dialog box that opens.

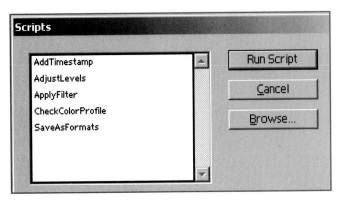

However you are not limited to using the scripts that were installed by default in the application. In the Photoshop Scripting 1.0 folder included in the download, you'll notice that an additional folder called **Sample Scripts** was created within it. The contents of this folder are dependent on your platform. If you're working with a Mac, there is an AppleScript and JavaScript folder, whereas if you are on the Windows platform, you'll find a JavaScript and Visual Basic folder.

As the JavaScript scripts are cross-platform and run from the Script option on the Automate sub-menu, we'll focus on these scripts for the moment. There are two methods by which you can access these or any other additional JavaScripts that you create:

- Choose the Browse option from the Scripts dialog box and then navigate through your hard drive to the location of these scripts.

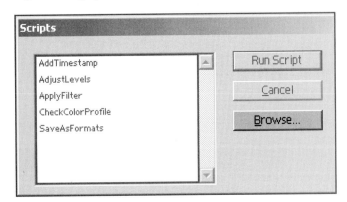

● If you want the additional scripts to be displayed automatically in the Scripts dialog box, you'll need to copy them into the Presets\Scripts folder within the Photoshop 7 application folder. Once they have been copied into the folder, they will be displayed alphabetically within the Scripts dialog box.

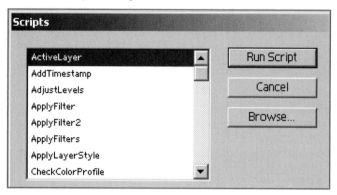

Writing and debugging JavaScripts for Photoshop

As mentioned in a previous section of this chapter, all you need to create your JavaScripts is a basic text editor – either Simple Text on the Mac or Notepad on the Windows platform will work perfectly well. You need to remember to save the file with a .js extension.

Once you have created a JavaScript file, you can use the JavaScript Debugging window from within Photoshop to step through the JavaScript code to check it. The Debugging window is accessed by holding down the OPT/ALT key and clicking on the **Debug Script** button, which appears instead of the **Run Script** option.

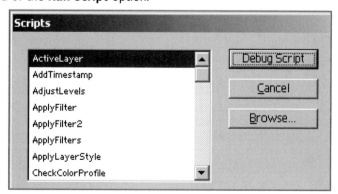

With the JavaScript Debugger window displayed, you can use the 'video controls' to move through the script checking with all debugging output being displayed in the upper-right hand pane of the window. More in-depth information can be found about using the debugger in the PS 7.0 Scripting Guide.pdf, page 27, located in the Documentation folder within the Scripting Support folder.

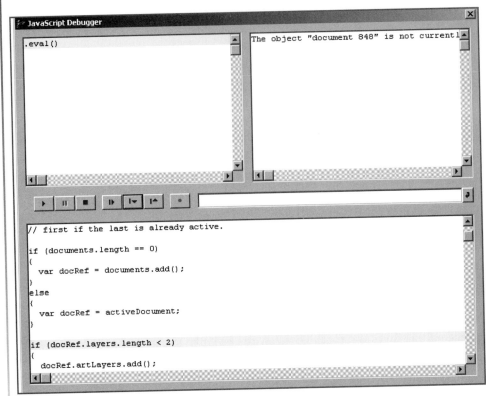

Using Visual Basic and AppleScript scripts

Although the focus of this chapter has been on using JavaScripts from within Photoshop, you are not limited to using just this scripting language. If you are on the Mac, using AppleScript, or on the Windows platform, using Visual Basic, will enable you to build complex scripts which function from outside of Photoshop.

Using either of these scripting languages means that you can create workflows that target not only specific Photoshop images, but also multiple hosts and applications.

There are extensive pdf files relating to using these scripting languages contained within the download folders.

Macintosh Requirements

If you wish to write AppleScripts that target applications including Photoshop, you'll need the following:

- Photoshop 7 must be installed as any system that is capable of running Photoshop 7 will support scripting.

- AppleScript and the Script Editor application must also be installed.

- For complex scripts, you may find that you'll need a more powerful third-party script editor for debugging.

Windows Requirements

On the Windows platform, Visual Basic is used to write these complex scripts that target more than one application in a workflow. You'll need the following installed on your machine:

- As with the Mac, you'll need to have Photoshop 7 installed because systems that can run Photoshop 7 will support scripting.

- Windows Scripting Host, Microsoft Visual Basic, or an application that contains a Visual Basic editor.

Using the ScriptingListener

There will be times when you wish to write scripts that are not possible to write using any of the scripting languages available, because they target features or functions that are not directly accessible within the language.

To overcome this limitation, you can use the Action Manager and the ScriptingListener plug-in file located in the Utilities folder within Photoshop Scripting 1 folder. The ScriptingListener plug-in functions in a manner similar to recording an action, except that instead of the steps appearing in the Action palette, they are recorded to a file with scripting code which matches the actions that you performed.

If you are working on a Mac, a `ScriptingListenerJS.log` file will be created on the Desktop, whilst on the Windows platform, a `C:\ScriptingListenerJS.log` file is created. Both of these files will contain the JavaScript code matching the actions performed. Additionally on the Windows platform, a `C:\ScriptingListenerVB.log` file containing the corresponding Visual Basic script will be saved. You can then edit these in the text editors mentioned above.

In order to use the ScriptingListener plug-in, it must be copied in the Photoshop 7.0\Plug-Ins\Scripting folder. However, having the plug-in installed when you do not need it to be running can degrade the performance of your machine and also create large unnecessary text files on your hard drive.

Conclusion

Although this chapter has only been a superficial look at the power of scripting and its usefulness for automating your Photoshop production workflow, there is so much more that can be learned, especially if you are a novice to scripting. As mentioned earlier, start out deconstructing and amending the sample scripts, and move on to writing those short scripts and testing them. As your knowledge and confidence grows, you'll find you will soon be developing more and more complex scripts.

Scripting support is a great step towards harnessing the full power of Photoshop 7, enabling you to work with greater speed and efficiency.

Chapter 14

Using Data Driven Graphics and Workgroup Management

What we'll cover in this chapter:

- The concept of Data Driven Graphics

- Understanding variables

- Defining variables in ImageReady

- Creating and modifying Data Sets

- Previewing Data Sets

- The concept of Workgroup Management with WebDAV

- Logging on and off WebDAV servers

- Checking In and Checking Out files

- Verifying, updating, and saving managed files.

The very term "Data Driven Graphics" hints at a departure from the traditional Photoshop / ImageReady territory – the creation and manipulation of imagery. This new inroad into the delivery and management of web-based graphics reflects the growing appreciation of the power of data driven websites and systems in general.

Data driven websites

But what is a data driven website? The worldwide adoption of the Internet as a vital business tool has elevated the web out of its early roots, where embedded images and static text were the norm, and repositioned it in a rapidly changing environment. The dynamics of world economies and volatile consumer buying trends call for a faster method for updating website information, and this is where data driven websites excel. Databases are used as the storage medium, storing countless numbers of individual items of data that can be rapidly searched for and retrieved. Data can be text or image based. Once a database has been populated with data, that data is at the disposal of the user. A typical data driven website may contain only a handful of pages, but have the ability to deliver many thousands of items of information. The pages themselves will be in the form of templates, and only these will appear in the user's browser. The information is stored on the database, and only that requested by the user will be searched for, retrieved, and delivered to the page template. This system is not only powerful in terms of how much information it can hold, but is also easier to maintain than a traditional static website would be, meaning it can be kept up-to-date with minimal effort.

This concept provides the impetus behind ImageReady's data driven graphics. Any web page requiring multiple image layouts in a common format would serve as an example, but web banner adverts and product display pages in particular would benefit from implementing data driven graphics.

Let's look at a typical scenario. This picture is a section from a travel company website. This is one of many dozens of standardized banners that appear throughout the site. Every few days the travel offers change, requiring a different photo and strap line. Different travel locations work on different profit margins, so in some cases the 15% online discount will not be offered and the discount icon will have to be removed. So within these small banners alone there are dozens of changes to be made each week, leaving the designer with a laborious and time-consuming task.

The ImageReady solution to this is to create the psd file only once. Any element requiring updating will be on its own layer and will be defined as a **Variable**. We will look at variables in more depth shortly, but basically they allow the defined element to be replaced by another element of the same type – for instance a photograph can be replaced by another photograph, or a text line by another text line. Rather than physically inserting the new element into place in the psd file, a script can be used to link to the database, where all the elements are stored, and the new psd will be generated automatically. (For more information on Scripting, see Chapter 13).

Using a script is just one way of linking the variables to the database. The web production application, Adobe GoLive can also be used, as well as the new dynamic image server software by Adobe called AlterCast. AlterCast provides a powerful solution to updating web graphics. As well as linking the variables specified in ImageReady to the database, it can also output the required optimized files such as jpg or gif and post them to the web. This function is performed by way of a script, which would have been created by the developer. The important thing is that designers can get on with designing and image creation, and programmers and developers can get on with creating scripts and maintaining databases.

The concept of variables

The only programming element designers need to have an understanding of is the term **Variables**. The word itself has associations with JavaScript and other programming languages but it can be applied to any real life situation.

A variable can be thought of as a container. The container is given a name, usually a name that describes what the container will hold. For example, a CD rack will contain CDs. The CD rack itself is of little value, so the contents, which are of course CDs in this case, become known as the value. This value will change depending how many CDs I am storing at any time.

Applying this principle to computer languages, we can use the example of a simple calculator, as used on a shopping website. We need the checkout page to automatically add up the total cost of all the widgets purchased and display this to the customer. We don't know in advance how many widgets the customer will buy, and we don't know the actual cost of the widget as the price fluctuates. So variables come to the rescue.

- We create a variable (the container) named Quantity. This holds the amount of widgets purchased, so the quantity becomes the value held within this variable.

- Next we create a variable named Price. When the customer types in the price, this will become the value held in the Price variable.

- Finally we need to create a variable that will display the total cost to the customer, so we create a variable named Total. In the programming language being used we can write a script that says:

  Multiply the value held in the variable named Quantity by the value in the variable named Price and display the result in the variable named Total.

We are left with the result of the calculation displayed on screen.

We can now apply this principle to the way variables have been implemented in ImageReady.

Take a look at the previous travel image again. We know the travel location photograph is going to change, so we can tell the layer on which the photo resides to make the pixels a variable. We can do the same for the strap line at the bottom of the image as that will change to reflect the picture and finally the same for the discount logo.

Let's run through the process in detail using the travel guide image as a working example.

The construction of the image is important. Every item that you want to be a variable **must be on its own layer**, separate from the background layer. How the Layers palette is set up relating to our working image is shown:

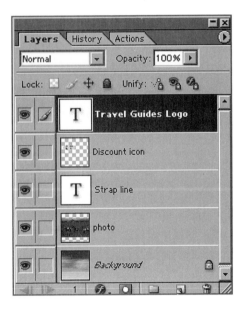

There are three kinds of variables in ImageReady. These refer to the kind of element you wish to change.

- **Pixel replacement variable** – used to change the pixel area of a layer. This one can be used to change the photo on the photo layer.

- **Text replacement variable** – used to replace a string of text in a text layer. This will be used to change the strap line.

- **Visibility variable** – used to show or hide a layer's content. This can be used to hide the discount icon when not applicable.

Defining a pixel replacement variable

If you want to use our file to go through these processes, it is called `Travelguides.psd` and can be downloaded from www.friendsofed.com, along with `surf.psd`, which will be used as our replacement image.

Select the layer for which you want to define a variable. (Variables cannot be defined for the background layer). First, I am going to define a variable for the photo layer, so the photo layer is selected.

Do either of the following:

- Go to Image > Variables > Define.

- From the pop up menu in the Layers palette select Variables.

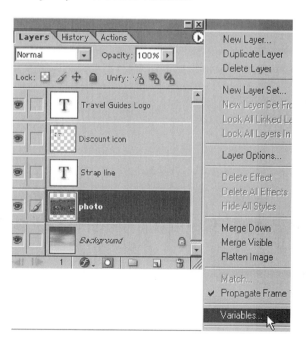

The Variables dialog box opens.

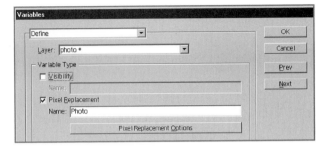

As we are defining a variable, leave Define as the option in the first drop down box. We will examine the other options later.

The **Layer** drop down box will show all the layers apart from the background layer. I have selected the layer called photo. The asterisk appearing in this drop down box denotes that this layer has been defined as a variable.

To make the pixel area (our photo) replaceable, check the **Pixel Replacement** checkbox.

The **Name** field refers to the variable name. Though not essential, you will find it helpful to use a name relevant to the element you want to change. In this case I have named the variable Photo. Naming of variables follows a strict convention. Names must begin with a letter, an underscore, or a colon. They must not contain spaces or special characters apart from periods, hyphens, underscores, or colons.

Next click the button labeled **Pixel Replacement Options**.

This dialog box allows you to define how the replacement image will be scaled, assuming the replacement is not the same size as the original.

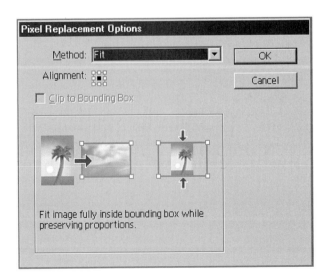

The available options are:

- **Fit** – scales the image to fit within the bounding box of the original image. This may result in part of the bounding box area being left empty.

- **Fill** – scales the image to completely fill the bounding box. This may result in the image extending beyond the bounding box. Select the **Clip to Bounding Box** check box to clip areas of the image that fall outside the bounding box.

- **As Is** – to prevent any scaling. Select the Clip to Bounding Box check box to clip areas of the image that fall outside the bounding box.

- **Conform** – scales the image non-proportionally to fit within the bounding box. This can result in the image becoming distorted.

In each case click a handle on the Alignment icon to define how the image should be aligned within the bounding box. Center is the default.

Click OK to confirm both dialog boxes.

A variable for the photo layer has now been defined.

Later we will look at how to define a **Data Set**, which will be used to specify the replacement image.

Defining a text replacement variable

The text on the strap line layer will also need to change, so I am going to define that layer as a variable as well.

Select the text layer, and use the same steps as for the pixel replacement variable to open the Variables dialog box.

Because the selected layer was a text layer, the **Text Replacement** check box is checked automatically. I have named the variable Strap_line, following the required naming convention.

Click OK to confirm the new variable.

Defining a visibility variable

Finally, to hide the 15% discount icon when it does not apply, a Visibility variable will be defined.

As before select the relevant layer and bring up the variables dialog box.

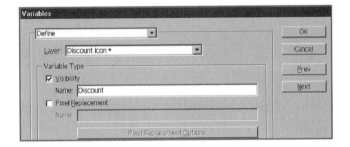

Check the **Visibility** check box. I have named the variable Discount. Click OK to confirm the settings.

All three kinds of variables have now been defined within the file: Pixel Replacement, Text Replacement, and Visibility.

Working with Data Sets

In order to specify the required changes to be made to the variables you have defined, you must create a **Data Set**. A Data Set describes a collection of variables and the data that is associated with the variables. By using different Data Sets, different images, text strings, and visibility settings can be uploaded to the template.

Editing the default Data Set

As soon as the first variable has been defined in the psd file, the default Data Set is created. For this reason it is not possible to edit the default Data Set until a variable has been defined.

To edit the default Data Set, go to Image > Variables > Data Sets.

Alternatively you can use the pop up menu button in the Layers palette and choose the Variables option as you did earlier. When the Variables dialog box opens, select **Data Sets** from the first drop down box.

The Variables dialog box pictured below appears displaying the default Data Set, named 'Data Set 1'. All functions relating to Data Sets can be performed in this box, including creating, editing, saving, and deleting Data Sets.

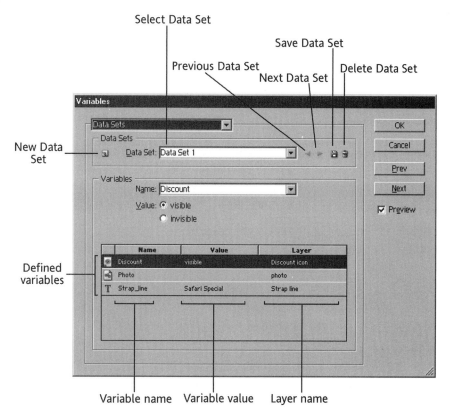

All the variables that have been defined in this Photoshop document (psd) file appear displaying their variable name, the variable value (if one has been used), and the layer name.

Remember, the creation of this Data Set is an automatic function as soon as you define your first variable, so nothing else remains to be done as far as this Data Set is concerned.

Creating a new Data Set

To replace the existing text and images with different ones, I am going to create a new Data Set, which will be associated with the variables that have been defined in the psd image.

Use the same steps as before to open the Variables dialog box. You will be looking at the same window as shown previously.

Click the **New Data Set** icon as labeled. This action causes Data Set 2 to appear in the Data Set drop down box. Notice also that the Previous and Next Data Set buttons have become enabled as more than one Data Set now exists.

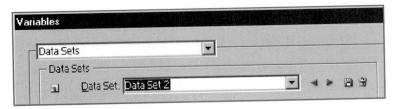

Numerically naming Data Sets will become confusing as the number grows, so a relevant name can be typed in the drop down box to identify what the Data Set refers to.

Now that the new Data Set has been created and named, the variables can have new values applied to them, thereby updating the image.

As shown in the image below, I named the Data Set 'Surf' and then clicked the variable called Discount, which becomes selected. This is the 15% discount icon. The original value of this variable was visible. Clicking the **invisible** radio button changes the value and will hide the layer.

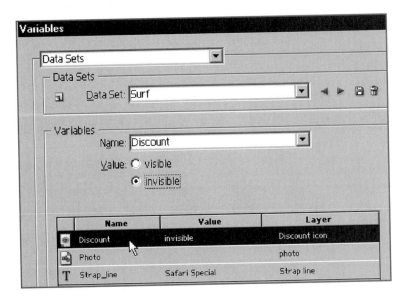

Next I needed to specify a different photo for the Surf Data Set. I selected the variable named Photo. Next to the Value field a Browse button appears. Click the button and navigate to the image you want to use. My image is called `Surfer.psd` and now appears in the Value field.

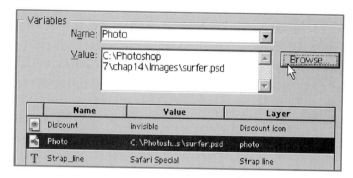

Finally the strap line variable value needs to change to reflect our new photo. Selecting the strap line variable enables you to type a new text string in the Value box as in the picture below. I typed the words "Dream Surf".

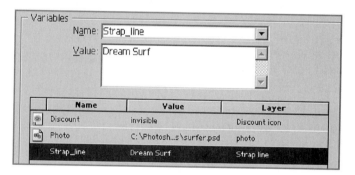

All that remains is to save the new Data Set. Click the **Save Data Set** icon. Click OK to close the dialog box.

Previewing Data Sets

ImageReady allows you to preview the Data Sets just as if they had been updated from the database.

From the toolbox, click the Preview document button or press the keyboard shortcut – Y.

The Tool Options bar now displays a drop down box containing all the Data Sets that have been created. Click the drop down arrow and select the Data Set you wish to preview. I selected the Surf Data Set.

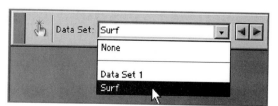

And this is the result. The updated image shows the new surf picture, the new text string 'Dream Surf', and the discount icon is now hidden.

Different Data Sets can also be selected and previewed by clicking the forward and back buttons next to the Data Set drop down box.

To leave preview mode and return to the original document, either click the same preview button, press Y or the Esc key, or click the cancel preview button in the tool option bar.

Modifying Data Sets

Over time you may want rename, edit, or delete data sets.

- **Renaming a data set** – from within the Variables dialog box, enter the new name in the Data Set field.

- **Changing the data in a data set** – from within the Variables dialog box, select the Data Set in which you want to change the data, then select the relevant variable and edit the value as required. Click the Save icon to update the change.

- **Deleting a data set** – from within the Variables dialog box, select the Data Set you want to delete and click the waste bin icon.

Workgroup management with WebDAV

Any working environment involving teams of people working on common projects, where information and files are shared, requires some kind of workgroup management. Workgroup management describes the operation and control of one team member passing files to another team member, ensuring only one person can edit a file at one time.

WebDAV (Web Distributed Authoring and Versioning) is a server technology supported by Photoshop. This technology can be used to connect to a WebDAV server, and from there, to manage files within the workgroup and prevent unintentional overwriting of files.

When using a WebDAV server, workgroup management is conducted via the web, allowing designers and developers to work as an efficient team even when they are geographically disparate. Any files being managed by the WebDAV server are permitted to be downloaded by all members of the team, but only one person can **check out** the file. Checking out a file means only the person who checked it out can edit the file. Other team members can still download the file but cannot edit it until the file has been **checked in** again. This system ensures that the file is always accessible without the risk of it being inadvertently overwritten.

To be able to use Photoshop's workgroup management you need to be able to connect to a WebDAV server. It is not the intention here to cover the setting up of a WebDAV server, but to introduce the essentials of how to manage, locate, check in, and check out files.

The first step is to set up the workgroup management preference.

Go to Edit > Preferences > File Handling.

The bottom half of the dialog box is the relevant section.

Check the **Enable Workgroup Functionality** check box to display the workgroup pop up menu at the bottom of the Photoshop window.

From the **Check Out from Server** drop down box you have the following choices:

- **Never** – opens the local copy of the file without checking it out and without displaying a dialog box.

- **Always** – automatically checks out the file when you open it.

- **Ask** – opens a dialog box when you open a file that has not been checked out.

From the **Update from Server** drop down box select one of the following:

- **Never** – opens the local copy of the file without displaying a dialog box and without downloading the latest version of the file from the server.

- **Always** – downloads the latest version of the file from the server without offering further options.

- **Ask** – opens a dialog box asking if you want to download the latest version.

Logging on to WebDAV servers

The method for logging on to WebDAV servers differs depending on the server. Check with your IT administrator for precise authentication procedures. In some cases a user name and password will need to be entered for every transaction. Alternatively, authentication may be required only once per session. In either case, type your user name and password into the authentication dialog box when it is displayed.

Logging off all WebDAV servers

Go to File > Workgroup > Logoff All Servers.

Opening managed files from the WebDAV server

When you want to view a managed file, you can open a copy of the file from the WebDAV server. This action creates a copy of the file on your hard drive and becomes known as a local copy.

Go to File > Workgroup > Open. Select the server and file you wish to open then either:

- Click Check Out to open and check out the file at the same time.

- Click Open to open a local copy without checking it out.

Reverting a checked out file to the version on the server

Once a local copy of the file has been created on your hard drive, if it is a checked out file you can revert it to the version of the file on the server.With the local copy of the file open, go to File > Workgroup > Revert.

Updating a non-checked out file from the version on the server

If it is a non-checked out file, you can update it with changes from the file on the server.

With the local copy of the file open, go to File > Workgroup > Update.

(If you decide to update or revert to the local copy, the action discards all changes made to the file.)

Checking Out a file

Checking out a file would be the desired approach. This will stop other team members from editing the file on the WebDAV server. Use either of the following methods depending on whether or not the file is open.

- If the file is already open, go to File > Workgroup > Check Out.

- If the file has not yet been opened, go to File > Workgroup > Open. Navigate to the desired file and click Check Out.

Verifying if a local file is available for check out

Open your local copy of the file.

Go to File > Workgroup > Verify State.

Checking In a file

When you have finished working on the file, you can check in the file to update the changes to the server and so permit the managed file to be checked out by other team members.

- Go to File > Workgroup > Check In to check in the file and update changes to the server.

- Go to File > Workgroup > Cancel Check Out to check in the file without updating changes to the server

Saving changes to the server

While you are working on a checked out file, you are able to save changes to the managed file on the server, allowing other team members to view your changes without releasing your lock on the file.

With your local copy of the file open go to File > Workgroup > Save.

Adding files to the server

When you add a file to a WebDAV server you are automatically creating a managed file.

With the file to be added to the server open, go to File > Workgroup > Save As. Select the server from the pop up menu and navigate to the directory where you want to save the file. Enter a name for the file in the Name text box, and then select a format from the Format pop up menu. If the file will be downloaded to a computer using a Windows operating system make sure the file name has an extension.

If you want to check out the file immediately, select **Keep This File Checked Out for Editing**. Finally, click Save.

Conclusion

In working environments that harness the power of database connectivity you will find ImageReady's tools for data driven graphics a designer's dream. The tedium of producing multiple identical image layouts has been eradicated by this version's provision of an imaginative solution, in the form of variables and Data Sets.

For designers working in a collaborative workgroup management system, Photoshop's support of WebDAV servers opens the door to an efficient and secure workflow system that utilizes the full ubiquity of the Web to ensure efficient project management, regardless of the team members' geographical locations.

Appendix

Upgraded Features From Version 5/5.5

For those upgrading from version 5/5.5, this appendix details the main elements upgraded in version 6 and carried through into version 7, which have not been covered in the main section of this book.

Photoshop interface

Pictured below is the Photoshop version 7 interface:

Tool Options Bar   Palette Well

Tool options bar

Running along the top of the screen, this replaces the individual tool options palettes. All the options available in the palettes previously can now be accessed from this options bar. The options bar is context sensitive and changes to reflect the current selected tool.

Palette well

As an aid to freeing up screen space, palettes can be docked in the palette well by dragging the palette tab into the well. To use the palette, click the name tab and it pops open. Once the palette has been used it collapses automatically. Numerous palettes can be stored at any one time.

Layer Enhancements

The previous 99 layer limit has now been lifted and as many layers can be created as the storage space on your computer allows.

Layer Sets

If large numbers of layers are being used, layer sets provide an easy way to manage them. A layer set is simply a folder into which layers can be organized. The picture below shows two text layers that have been comprised as part of layer set 'Set 1'. The set can be expanded to work on individual layers or collapsed to provide more space in the palette.

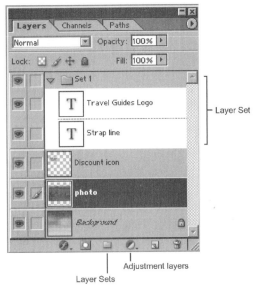

Adjustment layers can now be applied from the icon at the foot of the layers palette. Layers can also be color coded for easy identification.

Layer styles

Layer styles work in the same way as layer effects, applying preset effects such as beveling and shadows to a layer. The Layer Styles palette, pictured below, provides thumbnails of a range of styles that come with Photoshop.

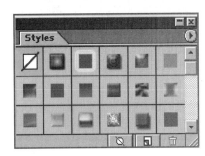

It is also possible to create your own combination of effects and save the combination as a style in this palette. All the steps that combine to make up a style appear in the Layers palette as sub layers. These sub layers, as shown below, can be double-clicked to open up the Layer Style dialog box where edits can be made.

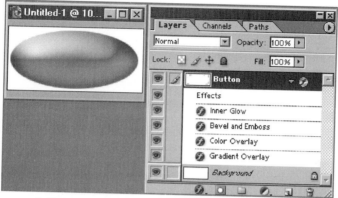

Toolbox additions and changes

The toolbox sees some minor changes and new tools.

Crop tool

Now occupying its own position rather than being within the Marquee Selection tools, the **Crop** tool (C) has also undergone a slight change in its operation. When the crop area has been defined, the outer remaining area can be dimmed, making it easier to make any final adjustments to the crop size.

Slice tool

For the Web, the **Slice** tool (K) allows you to define areas that will be sliced up into individual graphics, such as buttons in a navigation bar. The slices can then be optimized and the html generated all from within Photoshop.

Notes tool

Messages and general text information can be saved with the document in the form of a small notepad. Additionally, with a microphone you can also save voice messages.

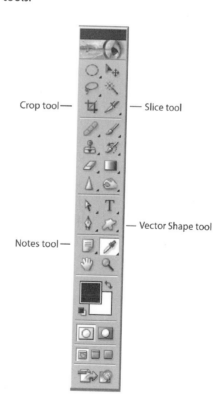

Crop tool — — Slice tool

— Vector Shape tool

Notes tool —

Vector Shape tool

The Vector Shape tool (U) creates a variety of basic shapes simulating the way a vector program such as Adobe Illustrator would work. The vector effect is achieved by way of a clipping path, which serves as a mask, known as a vector mask in Photoshop. As well as basic shapes being available such as ellipses and rectangles, you are able to combine and intersect shapes in a similar way to Illustrator pathfinders, resulting in highly complex shapes. The picture below is a combination of circles and rectangles, which have been combined to form the finished shape. The Layers palette displays the shape on its own layer along with the vector mask.

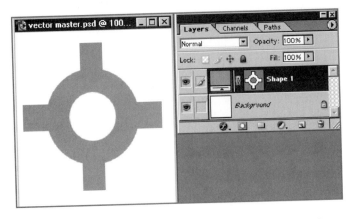

Vector shapes are fully scaleable without loss of quality and can be output to a postscript printer in the same way as conventional vector artwork.

Measure tool

The **Measure** tool (I) now resides in the same location as the Eyedropper tool.

Paint Bucket tool

The **Paint Bucket** tool (G) can be found in the same location as the Gradient tool

Text

Photoshop now has full vector text support. Text can also be typed directly onto the canvas rather than typing into a dialog box as before. Text remains live even when you apply one of the layer styles or the Warp text tool that distorts text, new to version 6.

Color Management

New Color Management options under Edit > Color Settings (SHIFT+CMD/CTRL+K) allow you to define **a Working Space** such as the Web, or different printing environments. A **Color Management Policy** in this dialog box allows you to specify how files with different profiles should be treated.

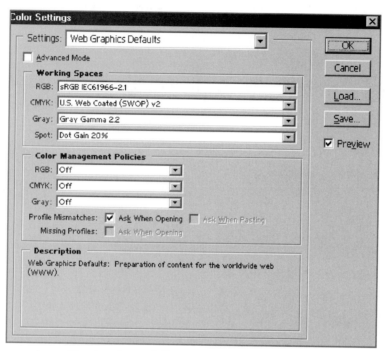

Once a color setting has been defined in Photoshop, it can be embedded in the file by clicking the check box in the Save dialog box.

Additional changes

- The Save a Copy option has now been merged with the Save As function.

- The Color Picker now displays hexadecimal values.

- When jumping into ImageReady from Photoshop, the document is automatically saved.

Index

Index

The index is arranged hierarchically, in alphabetical order, with symbols preceding the letter A. Many second-level entries also occur as first-level entries. This is to ensure that users will find the information they require however they choose to search for it.

Index

Notes

DESIGNER TO DESIGNER™

friends of ED writes books for you. Any suggestions, or ideas about how you want information given in your ideal book will be studied by our team.

Your comments are valued by friends of ED.

For technical support please contact support@friendsofed.com.

Freephone in USA: 800.873.9769
Fax: 312.893.8001

UK contact
Tel: 0121.258.8858
Fax: 0121.258.8868

Registration Code: | 087X42R5P4RYDA02

Photoshop 7.0 Upgrade Essentials – Registration Card

Name ....

Address ....

City ....State/Region ....

Country ....Postcode/Zip ....

E-mail ....

Profession: design student ☐ freelance designer ☐
part of an agency ☐ inhouse designer ☐
other (please specify) ....

Age: Under 20 ☐ 20-25 ☐ 25-30 ☐ 30-40 ☐ over 40 ☐

Do you use: mac ☐ pc ☐ both ☐

How did you hear about this book?....................................

Book review (name)....................................

Advertisement (name) ....

Recommendation ....

Catalog ....

Other ....

Where did you buy this book? ....

Bookstore (name) ....City....................................

Computer Store (name)....................................

Mail Order....................................

Other....................................

How did you rate the overall content of this book?
Excellent ☐ Good ☐
Average ☐ Poor ☐

What applications/technologies do you intend to learn in the near future?....................................
....

What did you find most useful about this book? ....
....

What did you find the least useful about this book? ....
....

Please add any additional comments ....
....

What other subjects will you buy a computer book on soon?
....
....

What is the best computer book you have used this year?
....
....

Note: This information will only be used to keep you updated about new friends of ED titles and will not be used for any other purpose or passed to any other third party.

friendsof

DESIGNER TO DESIGNER™

NB. If you post the bounce back card below in the UK, please send it to:

friends of ED Ltd.,
30 Lincoln Road,
Olton,
Birmingham.
B27 6PA